Blessings,
Dee Levens

THE
LONG
LONG
NIGHT
The Story of Destiny

DEE LEVENS

WESTBOW
PRESS®
A DIVISION OF THOMAS NELSON
& ZONDERVAN

Edited by Jack L. Levens

WestBow Press books may be ordered through booksellers or by contacting:

WestBow Press
A Division of Thomas Nelson & Zondervan
1663 Liberty Drive
Bloomington, IN 47403
www.westbowpress.com
1 (866) 928-1240

ISBN: 978-1-5127-6393-5 (sc)
ISBN: 978-1-5127-6392-8 (hc)
ISBN: 978-1-5127-6394-2 (e)

Library of Congress Control Number: 2016918891

Print information available on the last page.

WestBow Press rev. date: 11/22/2016

Contents

Preface: A Word to the Reader

If you are seeking God's purpose in your life, then *The Long, Long Night: The Story of Destiny* provides the blueprint for the path to your destiny. I welcome you to a compelling journey of intrigue, deception, commitment and love as you read this study of the book of Esther.

I encourage you to read each chapter of Esther in your Bible before you read the corresponding chapter in this book. All scriptures referenced or quoted in the body of the text came from the *New King James Version* of the Bible. Chapter 11 is an expression of my closing thoughts.

I have also placed a Study Guide: "Reflections and Talking Points" at the end of the book. This study guide will lead you to many reflective talking points which should create lively discussions among the participants in a study group.

Introduction

"For as the heavens are higher than the earth, so are My ways higher than your ways, and My thoughts than your thoughts." (Isaiah 55:9)

We will discover as we read and explore the book of Esther that Isaiah's words are interwoven throughout this story. We cannot in our present situation begin to comprehend the breadth of God's plan for us. His plan that He created specifically for us is one that our imagination could never envision.

My ten-year-old granddaughter once asked me, "Grandma, what would happen to me if my mother had married someone else?" Thankfully I had an idea what she meant by that question.

Taking a moment to carefully gather my thoughts, I simply explained to my granddaughter that she would not have been born. But God had a divine plan for her to be born and a destiny created by God especially for her life.

I further explained to her that no other set of parents could have brought her into this world. Only those two individuals that she calls Mom and Dad on that date and at that moment in time were destined to conceive her.

Continuing this timely conversation, I shared that even though her Mom and Dad were individually living out their own destiny, God used them as a married couple to bring into existence His plan for her. His plan for her life depended upon the obedience of her parents in following God's destiny for them.

After this interesting conversation ended, my granddaughter gave me a nod of understanding and, with an engaging smile, thanked me for answering her question. I took note of that moment as a seed planted and fruit to be produced at some future point in the life of my beautiful granddaughter.

If we could only grasp the eternal value that God places on our life. We so often think we have done nothing of any value or that our lives do not really matter. We may think God does not have a plan for us. But He does!

God has a divine plan for which you were individually created. One that far outreaches your thinking. Maybe someone of significant stature in your family will not appear for two, three or thirty generations, but *you* were a key to the birth of that leader.

Now, having told the story of my granddaughter, we will look at the book of Esther with the understanding that God says His thoughts are higher than our thoughts. Jeremiah 29:11 says, "For I know the thoughts that I think toward you, says the Lord, thoughts of peace and not of evil, to give you a future and a hope."

God desires to give us a future. But God's destiny for our life will only happen as we submit our own wills and our own desires to Him. He is the Potter and we are the clay (Isaiah 64:8).

Esther, Introduction/Background

The book of Esther is a story of strength, obedience, courage, and power. It covers such themes as political power, submission, honor, personal commitment, teamwork, love, hatred, sexism, racism, and much more.

It is generally suggested that the timeline of the events in the book appear to be around 483-472 BC.[1] Although the author of Esther is unknown, it is widely believed that the author was of Jewish origin and someone who would be familiar with the laws and customs of Persia. Two suggested writers are Mordecai or Ezra.[2]

While the book of Esther has been extensively studied and discussed, especially in women's groups, has it been examined to understand *why* it was written? Was it written primarily to encourage people of all faiths to not give up and to relentlessly contend for their faith? Or has it been investigated to look at the words and phrases as though they were secrets to be revealed?

My goal is to present the book of Esther as God told the prophet Ezekiel: "And the man said to me, 'Son of man, look with your eyes and hear with your ears, and fix your mind on everything I show you; for you were brought here so that

I might show them to you. Declare to the house of Israel everything you see." (Ezekiel 40:4) We will be searching for and examining the many nuggets that are so beautifully tucked into the book of Esther.

I want us to look first at why the book of Esther is so relevant to us today. The book of Esther does not directly mention God, the Holy Spirit, or Jesus even once throughout the entire book. Yet this short book reveals numerous insights and truths about the Holy Trinity that directly affect every Christian.

I found in my research that you cannot look at the Persian Empire history without Esther being a key part of the timeline. Queen Esther is not a fictional character, a fable, a parable, or just a great figure in a fascinating story.

Esther was a modest but beautiful young lady who was called into action by God, through the words of her cousin Mordecai, to represent and advocate for her people, the Jewish people, God's chosen race.

Do you recall what is the most common and significant quote from the book of Esther? One that you have heard in so many sermons and probably seen posted on cards and banners? Esther 4:14 says, "Yet who knows whether you have come to the kingdom for such a time as this?"

I feel certain that anyone who has attended church for any length of time can tell you the quote "for such a time as this" refers to Esther. It is the quote that keeps this book alive and provides the foundation for so many challenging sermons.

Although "for such a time as this" is a powerful quote, I want us to look not only at this one verse but carefully examine the life-changing message of the entire book of Esther.

Let me take a few minutes to introduce the primary players and present a brief background on each one. Please note there will be many opportunities in this study of Esther to draw spiritual comparisons between these individuals and some spiritual figures of the Bible.

Queen Vashti is one of the main characters in chapter 1. She was beautiful, extremely powerful among the women of the nation, strong willed, and probably a very dignified woman. She would not bend to the demand of King Ahasuerus to flaunt her publicly no matter what it meant to her personally. Queen Vashti was soon replaced by Esther.

As a side note here, recall our opening verse in Isaiah 55:9 that tells us that God's ways are higher than ours. God is actively creating opportunities all around us that set the stage for His plan to be implemented through His children who choose to be in His will. He always sets things in place *before* He sends us into battle. Remember that. He sets things in place *first*.

Back to describing Queen Vashti, it does not appear that she was an incompetent or unworthy queen deserving to be deposed from her throne. She simply was not the one God had destined at this timeline in history to play a pivotal key role in His eternal plan.

King Ahasuerus is often referred to in history as King Xerxes I who reigned over one hundred twenty-seven provinces from India to Ethiopia. His kingdom palace was located in Shushan the citadel just east of the Persian Gulf. The setting or timeline in the book of Esther begins in King Ahasuerus's third year of rule.

King Ahasuerus often sought counsel among those who were closest to him, and often granted power and authority to those in his inner circle. We will discover that he was known to make decisions, including impulsive decisions, based upon the suggestions and influence of others.

Memucan was one of the wise men closest to the king. It is also thought by some that Memucan and Haman were one and the same person.[3]

Haman was an evil man who thirsted for power. He was close enough to King Ahasuerus to give counsel to him. He often appears to have easily influenced or outright manipulated the king. He was greedy, vengeful, bitter, conniving, and just plain evil. Please note the character of Haman and compare it to that of Satan. We will reveal much more of the character of Haman as we examine the book of Esther.

Mordecai, Esther's elder first cousin, was of the lineage of Kish, a Jew, who we read about in 1 Chronicles 8:33 and Esther 2:5.

Take note of Kish's lineage recorded in 1 Chronicles 8:33: "Ner begot Kish, Kish begot Saul, and Saul begot Jonathan, Malchishua, Abinadab, and Esh-Baal."

Now notice the lineage of Mordecai found in Esther 2:5: "In Shushan the citadel there was a certain Jew whose name was Mordecai the son of Jair, the son of Shimei, the son of Kish, a Benjamite."

Why talk about Kish when we are trying to introduce Mordecai? I am a strong believer that the influence of the family and the lineage is a very powerful influence upon a child.

Mordecai's family history helped shape the values and character of Mordecai. Kish was the father of King Saul, so Mordecai was of the royal Jewish lineage of King Saul. I would tend to believe that Mordecai also knew of King David and Jonathan, Saul's son, and the other family members of the royal house.

We see how Mordecai happened to be living in Persia rather than in Israel or Judah in Esther 2:6: "Kish had been carried away from Jerusalem with the captives who had been captured with Jeconiah king of Judah, whom Nebuchadnezzar the king of Babylon had carried away."

Although Mordecai's lineage had been captured and relocated to Shushan the citadel, he is exactly where he is destined to be at this moment in time. As with Mordecai, there will be times when we will be far removed from our comfort zone when we are actively engaged in God's will.

Esther was the younger first cousin of Mordecai. Mordecai and Esther's fathers were brothers from the Jewish tribe of Benjamin. Esther's parents died and she became an orphan. Mordecai, who was older, adopted her as his own and loved her dearly. Esther grew up to be a charmingly beautiful young woman living under the guardianship and guiding influence of Mordecai.

Earlier I commented that family history is important. I imagine there were many lively discussions of the past family histories at the house of Mordecai concerning King Saul, Jonathan, and King David. Esther, by birth a young lady of royal descent, would have been included and probably participated in these family dialogues.

Some of the more intense conversations were likely about the captivity of their people and of the contempt and hostility towards them as a race. Mordecai may have spoken of the tragic experiences and frustrations of the Jewish people which were often a direct consequence of their disobedience to God.

If you only casually read the book of Esther, you will think this is just a fascinating Bible story about a sweet little orphan girl adopted by her noble cousin Mordecai. But not so! This compelling story of Esther emerges as "The Story of Destiny."

～ Chapter 1 ～

The Queen Said "NO!" (483 BC)

The setting in the book of Esther took place during the time of King Ahasuerus. It begins with King Ahasuerus hosting a grand feast designed to pompously display all his vast wealth and majestic splendor to the princes and nobles in his kingdom.

You might question the motive driving the king's decision to throw such an extravagant party. There was always political unrest among the countries and rulers would pounce on weakness.

King Ahasuerus wanted to demonstrate to surrounding countries that he was still in total command. He would certainly be making a public political statement of his enormous wealth and power with such a festive banquet in his vast kingdom.

After six long months of feasting and boasting, the king then hosted a separate feast, lasting seven days, for all the people who were present in Shushan, the capital. This party was given in the court of the garden of the king's royal palace.

At the same time the king's lavish party was being held, Queen Vashti was also hosting a feast for the women in the royal palace (Esther 1:9).

On the seventh day of the king's feast the king decided to present his beautiful Queen Vashti to all the people of his party. Having already displayed to everyone his possessions, his land, and his palaces, what was left? His beautiful queen!

It appears the king exercised poor judgement because it was an utter insult in their customs for the king's queen to be displayed in public in this manner. It was also obvious he wanted to show her off as a possession of his, not as his highly respected queen. Queen Vashti refused to go with the king's eunuchs who had been ordered to go to her chambers and bring her to his party.

This blatant refusal by the queen created royal embarrassment for the king in his own palace. The king beckoned his wise men who understood the situation and the culture and sought their counsel.

Notice which wise man responded first with a solution before the others could say anything. We observe that this same wise man also urged the king to issue a royal decree so that the proposed solution, or the plan, could not be altered under the Medes and Persian law.

This bold wise man, Memucan, addressed in Esther 1:13-22, is believed by some scholars to be the same person as Haman who appears later in this story using this same devious tactic.[1]

Queen Vashti's refusal to obey the king's command to come to his party "to show her beauty to the people, and the officials" had created quite a public and political embarrassment for him (Esther 1:12). He felt that he had lost respect among his own servants, the princes and guests, and his countrymen.

King Ahasuerus desperately needed a response to regain respect as the king. Memucan, speaking for the wise men, gave the king counsel to issue a royal decree to have Queen Vashti removed as royal queen and to give her royal position "to another who is better than she" (Esther 1:16-20).

Included within the decree that deposed Vashti as queen was a letter to be sent to all provinces that crushed the inner spirit of each woman by declaring that each man should be master in his own house, and to speak in the language of his own people.

These letters clearly defy God's intentions for the marital relationship. God sends out words of love and respect to the woman. He placed the woman under the husband concerning her position within the marriage, but not as a slave.

What does Satan want to do with a marriage that is blessed by God? Satan wants to steal and destroy the *joy* of the relationship. He wants to stop the communication between the husband and wife. Satan wants to kill, steal, or destroy the marriage.

God has not stopped the wife's voice, her thinking, her abilities to serve, or to be creative. These letters written by Memucan were meant to destroy the mutually supportive relationship enjoyed by husbands and wives. Memucan's plot to steal the joy of the relationship was shrewdly disguised in the form of a royal decree issued at the end of chapter 1.

Before we journey into chapter 2, I want to uncover some possible symbolism contained within this first chapter.

First let us examine the reference to vessels, drinking, and royal wine.

> And they served drinks in golden vessels, each vessel being different from the other, with royal wine in abundance, according to the generosity of the king. In accordance with the law, the drinking was not compulsory; for so the king had ordered all the officers of his household, that they should do according to each man's pleasure. (Esther 1:7-8)

Often in the New Testament the word *vessel* is used as a reference to the body as a spiritual container, a dwelling place where the Holy Spirit abides (1 Corinthians 6:19).

I find it very inspirational that each of us are created by God with our own unique DNA and thumbprint. Each vessel is different and handmade by God. We are uniquely and wonderfully made.

Psalm 139:14 declares, "I will praise You, for I am fearfully and wonderfully made; Marvelous are Your works, and that my soul knows very well."

At the king's banquet the guests were offered an abundance of royal wine according to the generosity of the king. When we, as living vessels created by God, accept Jesus Christ as our Savior and Lord, we are filled with the Holy Spirit (which I like to refer to as the Royal Wine) and yes, it is according to the King's generosity (John 3:16).

In accordance with the law, drinking was not compulsory. The officers of the household were to serve drinks according to each man's pleasure. Please note that it was not the king nor the law that prevented anyone from drinking all the royal wine that they wanted. It was the *choice* of the holder of the drink.

I have often heard, "Well, if God wanted me to be filled with the baptism of the Holy Spirit, He would give it to me." That is a myth, and it does not come from God. You are the one who must ask for more and for refills (Luke 11:13).

Personally, I just love standing under the pitcher of Royal Wine with my mouth wide open. I want to receive so much Royal Wine that my vessel begins to spill over. It has been and always will be my choice whether I drink of the Royal Wine.

If you look at the cup of communion in the New Testament in Matthew 26:28, you will see that the blood of Jesus Christ was shed for our forgiveness. Many will accept salvation from Jesus as an entrance into heaven. But a great number of those will never dive into the depths of life that He desires for them to have because they will not accept the fullness of the forgiveness that He offers to them.

They continue to believe Satan's lie that, because of their sinful past, they are now unworthy of His love and forgiveness. So many simply cannot comprehend how much Jesus has to offer through His unconditional love for them while they live here on this earth.

Salvation, as well as being baptized with the Holy Spirit, will never be imposed upon anyone. Everyone is invited to partake of this delicious Wine.

Jesus announced to His disciples that He had to go away in order for them to be baptized with the Holy Spirit (John 16:16-17). Then He instructed His disciples to go and tarry or wait with earnest expectation in Jerusalem until they were baptized with the Holy Spirit (Acts 1:4-8).

Being baptized with the Holy Spirit is that abundance or overflowing that Jesus is urging each one of us to seek. The Holy Spirit enters your life when you are first saved. Then, at your request for Jesus to impart all that He has for you, Jesus will baptize you in the Holy Spirit. You can have the Royal Wine of the Holy Spirit in abundance.

Having examined some of the symbolism in this chapter, let us now look closer at the decree and the key players involved.

"If it pleases the king, let a royal decree go out from him, and let it be recorded in the laws of the Persians and the Medes, so that it will not be altered, that Vashti shall come no more before King Ahasuerus; and let the king give her royal position to another who is better than she." (Esther 1:19)

Note that the Lord carefully arranges all the pieces together *before* revealing His own key players. Esther and Mordecai have not entered the scene yet. But the scenes that are yet to be written are already being prepared by God.

God does not put you in a position that He has not already prepared for you. Although the scenario may appear to be a difficult one to execute, remember that God put you there in His grand scheme for a purpose—divine purpose and destiny.

As discussed earlier, there was an inner circle that influenced King Ahasuerus in his decision making process. One of these influential men is revealed in Esther 1:14: "those closest to him being … and Memucan, the seven princes of Persia and Media, who had access to the king's presence, and who ranked highest in the kingdom."

An interesting assertion was found in Wikipedia, "According to the biblical book of Esther, Memucan was one of the seven vice-regents of the Persian King Ahasuerus. It is not stated in the text explicitly, but it is the generally accepted belief that Memucan and Haman were the same person."[2]

If Memucan and Haman are the same person as some scholars believe, pay close attention to his behavior and character as described in Esther 1:16-20. Memucan's style in proposing his persuasive solution to the king and his character mirrors that of Haman as we will discover later in the book.

Seizing the opportunity, Memucan asserts himself as the voice (or leader) among the seven vice-regents. He appears to be the one that can influence or manipulate King Ahasuerus with the plan that feeds the king's ego. The king heeds the counsel of Memucan and implements the royal decree.

I surmise that the king places his trust in Memucan. With his guard down, the king can easily be led down the intended path suggested by Memucan. Putting words in the king's mouth appears to give great delight to Memucan as he turns the king into his own puppet.

The king is quickly persuaded to implement Memucan's plan to remove Queen Vashti. We will discover in later chapters that the king also entertains Haman's plot and agrees with it as well. Memucan's and Haman's character and style do appear to have a lot in common as one would expect if they are the same person.

Earlier Memucan's decree to remove Queen Vashti was briefly discussed. Following the decree letters were dispatched as recorded at the end of chapter 1.

"Then he sent letters to all the king's provinces, to each province in its own script, and to every people in their own language, that each man should be master in his own house, and speak in the language of his own people." (Esther 1:22)

It is difficult to imagine or even understand why the king felt he needed to make a law that each man should be master of his own house and speak in the language of his own people. Upon further investigation we uncover some interesting information about these letters.

One piece of historical information is that the "letters" actually became a law. "If it pleases the king, let a royal decree go out from him, and let it be recorded in the laws of the Persians and the Medes, so that it will not be altered...." (Esther 1:19)

God had already ordained in scripture in Genesis 3:16 that the man should be the head of the woman. I find it extremely interesting that this royal decree restated what God had already spoken and was recorded in the laws of the Persians and Medes.

The Ten Commandments and the laws and traditions that we study in the first five books of the Old Testament were recorded by Moses and intended for the people of Israel, the Jews. But this royal decree and law was written by the Persians and Medes government—the *Gentile* government. As a result, no matter whether you are a Jew or a Gentile, the same law or principle as ordained by God is still in effect to this day.

Continuing our examination of this royal decree or letter, look at the phrase "master in his own house" found in Esther 1:22.

If you are a man, especially as a husband and father, the Lord will hold you accountable for this role within your home. Are you the master (in the model of Christ) in your own household? Do you lead or bring your family to the house of God? Do you submit your own authority to God's rule and Kingship?

The New Testament gives us the model for the husband-wife relationship in Ephesians 5:22-23 which says, "Wives, submit to your own husbands, as to the Lord. For the husband is head of the wife, as also Christ is head of the church; and He is the Savior of the body."

A few verses later in Ephesians 5:33 God tells us, "Nevertheless let every one of you in particular so love his own wife as himself; and let the wife see that she respects her husband."

Looking further into Esther 1:22, we read that the men are to speak in the language of their own people. So what language is spoken by your own people? Do you speak life or do you speak death? (Proverbs 18:21)

There are only two kinds of people in this world—those who claim Satan as their father and those who claim God as their Father.

To which people do you belong? Are you speaking life? Depending on your choice you will know which language is spoken inside your own house.

⌐ *Chapter 2* ⌐

The Installation of Queen Esther (478 BC)

Chapter 1 opened the way for Esther and Mordecai to enter the scene. Chapter 2 details their entry into the inner circle of the palace of King Ahasuerus and describes the process of celebrate the crowning of Esther as their new queen.

As we read these events unfolding we can reflect back on our own lives and see where God has brought us from, or out of, and where He is leading us now. When we do, we will see it is all by the grace of God, and that God had His hand upon our lives or we would not be here today. This was the case for both Esther and Mordecai.

Chapter 2, now four or five years after the end of chapter 1, starts off with King Ahasuerus reminiscing about the time when Queen Vashti refused to come to his banquet so he could display her beauty to all the guests. He also remembered his decree, suggested by Memucan, that Queen Vashti be removed from her position as his queen and the women of every household were to honor their husbands.

Esther 1:22 reads, "that each man should be master in his own house." Please note that man, not God, wrote that law. This secular law decrees that the man was to be the master in his own house and the woman is described more like that of a servant to the man than as a wife.

This arrangement is not the way God intended for a man and a woman to function in a marriage. They were to be equal in His sight. God set an order for marriage placing the man as head of the woman, but man was to submit himself to God as his head.

Both the man and the woman were to be submissive to someone else; the woman to the man and the man to God. Marriage works so much smoother when God's order of assignment or position is obeyed. God *is* love and the marriage must operate under the principle of a pure love or it will have divisions.

Here is what God planned for the man and woman. Genesis 1:27 reads, "So God created man in His own image; in the image of God He created him; male and female He created them."

> But for Adam there was not found a helper comparable to him. And the Lord God caused a deep sleep to fall on Adam, and he slept; and He took one of his ribs, and closed up the flesh in its place. Then the rib which the Lord God had taken from man He made into a woman, and He brought her to the man. And Adam said: 'This is now bone

of my bones and flesh of my flesh; she shall be called Woman, because she was taken out of Man.' Therefore, a man shall leave his father and mother and be joined to his wife, and they shall become one flesh. (Genesis 2:20-24)

Poor lonely King Ahasuerus must have complained to his servants because they are the ones who suggested the next plan of action for the king.

'Let beautiful young virgins be sought for the king; and let the king appoint officers in all the provinces of his kingdom, that they may gather all the beautiful young virgins to Shushan the citadel, into the women's quarters, under the custody of Hegai the king's eunuch, custodian of the women.... Then let the young woman who pleases the king be queen instead of Vashti.' This thing pleased the king, and he did so. (Esther 2:2-4)

It is worth noting that the king was approachable by individuals from any position or rank. First the seven vice-regents give counsel to the king. Now the servants of the king offer suggestions to him. God used both high and low positional people to set into motion His divine plan in the book of Esther.

Going back to the discussion of marriage, the termination of the relationship between King Ahasuerus and Queen Vashti is a snapshot of many marriages in our society today. When there is a squabble among the husband and the wife, in today's times, there is often a divorce. A decree is written against their unity. Then we often begin the search for the next person to fill the role of the first spouse.

This all too common and acceptable practice is not what God ordained. It is the way of the world and even the counsel of the world. It was the king's own advisors and servants who told him to remove Queen Vashti and to search for another queen.

It was not a prophet of God who came and counseled the king. God's counsel is found in Mark 10:8: "and the two shall become one flesh." Deep cuts or hurts occur when one flesh becomes two.

God will take a mess and give us a message if we are willing and available. God used this disorder in the king's palace to position His own child, Esther, in the king's palace as the newly crowned queen.

I do not believe God created the mayhem nor caused Queen Vashti to refuse the king's request to come to him when he commanded. But God did use this situation to speak to the king and to save a nation.

God takes what Satan means for harm and turns it into something good. As we read in the Bible, Joseph describes his suffering in Egypt after he was sold by his brothers into slavery. "But as for you, you meant evil against me; but God meant it for good, in order to bring it about as it is this day, to save many people alive." (Genesis 50:20)

The prophets of old studied the scriptures to determine the birth of Christ's timeline and location. We read in the New Testament gospels the story of Jesus' birth and the three wise men who followed the star to find Jesus in Bethlehem. These three wise men had been studying the old prophets. This was not hidden information to them. It was clearly written in the books of the prophets.

> 'But you, Bethlehem, in the land of Judah,
> Are not the least among the rulers of Judah;
> For out of you shall come a Ruler
> Who will shepherd My people Israel.' (Matthew 2:6)

I believe that if the three wise men could comprehend that one day a Savior, a King, would enter this world then how much more would Satan know that God was about to reveal to the world His plan for their salvation? Satan would naturally have his eyes and ears open to any movement upon the earth that signified the coming of the Savior.

We clearly see in the Old Testament that God consistently protected and preserved the Jewish people, His chosen race. Why did God divinely intervene on their behalf each time it looked like they were going to be totally destroyed?

The reason is simple but unmistakable. This was the chosen lineage through which the birth of His Son, Jesus Christ, was destined. I feel certain that Satan had set traps all along this Jewish lineage to try to stop the birth of Jesus Christ. Satan wanted to destroy the lineage of Jesus.

We discover evidence of Satan's traps through the creation of doubt and confusion when we examine closely the scriptures.

> Therefore many from the crowd, when they heard this saying, said, 'Truly this is the Prophet.' Others said, 'This is the Christ.' But some said, 'Will the Christ come out of Galilee? Has not the Scripture said that the Christ comes from the seed of David and from the town of Bethlehem, where David was?' So there was a division among the people because of Him. (John 7:40-43)

Satan tried to stop the birth of Christ by attempting to destroy an entire Jewish race. He failed and Jesus *was* born in Bethlehem just as the scriptures had declared! Even after Jesus was born in Bethlehem, Satan continued to try to create confusion among the people by twisting the scriptures in their minds as he still does today.

Getting back to our story, look how God in the following scriptures ushers in a Jew and positions the destined lineage of Jesus into the royal palace and ultimately into the presence of the king.

> In Shushan the citadel there was a certain Jew whose name was Mordecai the son of Jair, the son of Shimei, the son of Kish, a Benjamite. Kish had been carried away from Jerusalem with the captives who had been captured with Jeconiah king of Judah, whom Nebuchadnezzar the king of Babylon had carried away. And Mordecai had brought up Hadassah, that

is, Esther, his uncle's daughter, for she had neither father nor mother. The young woman was lovely and beautiful. When her father and mother died, Mordecai took her as his own daughter. So it was, when the king's command and decree were heard, and when many young women were gathered at Shushan the citadel, under the custody of Hegai, that Esther also was taken to the king's palace, into the care of Hegai the custodian of the women. (Esther 2:5-8)

Returning to our story we see that Esther is taken into the custody of Hegai, the king's custodian of the women. She obtains favor in Hegai's sight and he moves her into the finest quarters within the house of the women and gives her seven choice maidservants (Esther 2:9-11).

This all sounds so sweet. Esther has been given the most luxurious living arrangements, the seven choice maidservants, and matchless beauty preparations. She absolutely lacked nothing. But wait! She is still not free to simply walk away. She is virtually a captive of the king.

Just as Mordecai's family lineage had been held captive we now observe that Esther is also bound and constrained to the king. Mordecai is well aware of the stories he must have heard as a youth of the captivity of his own people.

Esther 2:11 reads, "And every day Mordecai paced in front of the court of the women's quarters, to learn of Esther's welfare and what was happening to her." Mordecai was very concerned about the well-being of Esther and did not abandon Esther even in her captivity.

This reminds me of the love and concern Jesus has for each one of us. Every day Jesus paces outside the door of our heart and waits for us until we let Him in.

In sin we are held captive by Satan. We cannot just walk away from our captor. We must have a Savior that can free us from the deathtrap of sin into which we are all born (Isaiah 42:6-7).

Revelation 3:20 tells us, "Behold, I stand at the door and knock. If anyone hears My voice and opens the door, I will come in to him and dine with him, and he with Me."

"Each young woman's turn came to go in to King Ahasuerus after she had completed twelve months' preparation, according to the regulations for the women, for thus were the days of their preparation apportioned: six months with oil of myrrh, and six months with perfumes and preparations for beautifying women." (Esther 2:12)

Esther was selected as a candidate and moved into the women's quarters. She then engaged in twelve long months of preparations. This process was required before placing her in line with the other women who were waiting to enter into the king's presence.

We may eventually be placed in a position of great responsibility, but we also learn that it may not come immediately. We may appear to be stagnant or going in circles when in fact God is preparing us for the journey ahead. He does not send us out on the mission until we are fully prepared.

Esther's preparation oils

One of the essential oils applied to Esther was myrrh. Myrrh is a type of resin that is bled from a number of thorny trees. The resin forms a natural gum, and it can be converted into an essential oil that is used in perfume, medicine and oral hygiene.

Myrrh has a balsamic odor and tastes bitter. Its name originates from the Arabic term murr, which means bitter. This very expensive oil is not only used for making perfume, incense, and medicine but also for anointing the dead.[1]

For the first six months Esther was required to have this balsamic and bitter tasting oil applied to her. Then for another six months she was anointed with other oils and perfumes for beautifying women of that time. The last six months may not have been any better for Esther than the first six months as far as odor or taste is concerned.

Over the years I have seen paintings and drawings of Esther engaged in this twelve-month period of preparation. She is often depicted bathing in a big bubble bath of oils and her maidservants are waiting on her every need.

Despite what the pictures attempt to portray, she was still a captive. Since oil of myrrh is also used for an embalming oil for burial, I wonder what might have been going on in the mind of Esther?

Esther's path to the throne as queen was not presented to her on a silver platter. She had to endure and successfully complete twelve long months of exhausting preparations—one long year.

We so often want God to use us in something important and instead we feel like we are just spinning our wheels. We are just floundering and doing nothing. Maybe we are having some oil of myrrh rubbed on us!

God is doing things in our lives that we cannot see and He is preparing us to be ready to enter the scene. But first we must patiently wait and be prepared for the day our name is called to continue our journey of destiny.

Esther 2:13-16 tells us that Esther did exactly as Hegai had counseled her and she obtained favor with everyone around her. Look at the timeline once again in verse sixteen. It was now the tenth month of the seventh year of the reign of King Ahasuerus.

Recall that Queen Vashti refused to obey him in the third year of his reign. So often we read a scripture and think that it all took place in a short period of time. Scripture reveals that this story plays out over a timespan of several years.

A significant moment occurs in Esther 2:17: "So he set the royal crown upon her head and made her queen instead of Vashti." The king chooses Esther over all the other candidates in his house.

The stage is now set for Esther who has been divinely placed in a critical position to make a difference. Now the next stage to be set is for Mordecai.

An extravagant celebration feast is given for Esther, The Feast of Esther. All the servants and all the people of the land celebrate the crowning of Esther as their new queen.

While at this celebration Mordecai overhears two of King Ahasuerus's doormen talking about a plot to kill the king. Mordecai reports this information to Esther who in turn informs the king in Mordecai's name. The matter is investigated, the report is confirmed, and the two men are hung for their crime against the king (Esther 2:18-23).

This incident, and Mordecai's bravery to get word to the king through Queen Esther, was recorded in the king's book of chronicles in the king's presence. Nothing else was done—*just a recording*. This simple recording that appears to be so insignificant will later prove to be the pivotal turning point in this story and the course of history.

—❧ *Chapter 3* ❧—

Haman's Great Revenge (474 BC)

"After these things King Ahasuerus promoted Haman, the son of Hammedatha the Agagite, and advanced him and set his seat above all the princes who were with him." (Esther 3:1)

It is easy to ignore a simple phrase like "After these things" in the above referenced scripture. There is no significant information within the phrase that catches our attention. Not included in that phrase is that four to five years passed before the king promoted Haman.

These are some of the significant moments or events that happened during these four to five years:

- Esther was placed in position as queen of Persia
- Mordecai exposed a plot designed to kill the king by two of the king's own men
- The two traitors were found guilty and hanged
- The saving of the king's life by Mordecai was recorded in the king's book of the chronicles

So "after these things" happened chapter 3 starts off with the king promoting Haman, the son of Hammedatha the Agagite. But before we continue the story let us refresh our memory with some of the facts the author of the book of Esther was so careful to include about the key characters.

- King Ahasuerus "reigned over one hundred twenty-seven provinces, from India to Ethiopia" (Esther 1:1). The writer was making sure we understood later in history which king was involved in this critical story of destiny.
- Mordecai "was a *certain Jew* whose name was Mordecai the son of Jair, the son of Shimei, the son of Kish, a Benjamite" (Esther 2:5-6). The writer then relates a brief history of Mordecai the Jew and his family.
- Esther is clearly listed as in the house of Mordecai through the bloodline of their fathers. Their fathers were brothers. Mordecai was her elder cousin.

The author of Esther gives great attention to the lineage of the key characters. Why so much detail on the lineage of these characters in a book that does not mention the name of God in any form even once? Why so much emphasis on the background of each of the characters? The answers to these questions will reveal the order and intimate detail that God requires for His divine plans to be accomplished.

Haman was a descendant of King Agag of the Amalekites. The Amalekites were a people who were commanded by God through the prophet Samuel to be utterly destroyed by King Saul and David. Look at 1 Samuel 15:1-35.

King Saul was sent by God on a mission to utterly destroy the Amalekites for their sins. Saul and his army were to destroy everything including all the women, children and animals. No spoils were to be taken.

But Saul listened to his people and they kept the best of the animals to "offer to Samuel's God." The prophet Samuel was very angry at Saul for his disobedience.

Saul further disobeyed God by bringing back alive the Amalekite King Agag with him. After a long discourse with King Saul, Samuel has King Agag brought to him and he takes his sword and chops him to pieces.

Samuel then spoke the familiar and often quoted scripture found in 1 Samuel 15:22: "Has the Lord as great delight in burnt offerings and sacrifices, as in obeying the voice of the Lord? Behold, to obey is better than sacrifice, and to heed than the fat of rams."

In Esther 3:1-2, it appears as though the king has promoted Haman to the highest position within his kingdom. It is also expected of the people within the king's gate to bow and pay homage to Haman.

But Mordecai would not bow or pay homage. We know what *bow down* means, but how about *pay homage*? Basically they are similar except I think pay homage means more of a bowing with appreciation, almost in a worshipful manner, to the one to whom you bow. In other words, I believe Haman wanted homage paid to him as though he were a god to be worshipped.

I believe this was just too much for Mordecai to swallow. He had already heard all the stories of King Nebuchadnezzar and his iron fisted style of rule. He had listened for years of the degrading conditions of his Jewish people while in captivity.

Mordecai was growing weary with all this feeling of captivity. Even his beloved Esther was now captive in her own way as queen of Persia. What else could they possibly want from him?

Mordecai had told Haman's nagging servants, who kept coming to him to tell him to bow to Haman, that he was not a Persian and not under the Persian law. He reminded them that he was a Jew under God's law. But, to the servants' way of thinking, if you walk within the king's gates, you are to obey the rule of the king. Makes sense to me. What about you?

So the servants constantly reported to Haman about that man who called himself a Jew and refused to pay homage (Esther 3:4). Now Haman begins to pay attention to this man that is not bowing.

We do not know just how familiar Haman was with Mordecai the Jew prior to the servants pointing Mordecai out to him. Perhaps Haman had never noticed Mordecai prior to his servants bringing it to his attention (Esther 3:5).

There is a message to be taught and a lesson to be learned from this situation. The servants stirred up contention with their reports about Mordecai. How easy it is to plant evil thoughts in the minds of others, especially when they are already filled with an evil and corrupt character.

Esther 3:6: "But he disdained to lay hands on Mordecai alone, for they had told him of the people of Mordecai. Instead, Haman sought to destroy all the Jews who were throughout the whole kingdom of Ahasuerus—the people of Mordecai."

Why was Haman not satisfied with just killing only Mordecai? I believe he too had a memory of his family's history.

Haman was of the lineage of King Agag, the one that King Saul was commanded by God to be killed when the Israelites had captured their lands and the Agagite people. But Saul had kept him alive and the prophet Samuel later had to kill him. In Haman's mind, the Jews and King Saul had killed his people.

Haman seized this opportunity to exact revenge on the Jewish people and began to plot this genocide plan in the name of his people. Through manipulation he would be able to forcibly obtain vengeance upon the Jewish race using the king's name.

But was the execution really being carried out in his own people's name? Or, was it personal? There is a big difference when you see the inside story of Haman and Mordecai. Haman is a classic example of the damage that bitterness and unforgiveness can do to a person or even to an entire race or culture.

Haman initiates his evil plan by establishing the execution date through a common practice as seen in Esther 3:7: "In the first month, which is the month of Nisan [March or April in the Gregorian calendar], in the twelfth year of King Ahasuerus, they cast Pur (that is, the lot), before Haman to determine the day and the month, until it fell on the twelfth month, which is the month of Adar [February or March in the Gregorian calendar]." The phrase *casting Pur* is now *casting lots* in our current day vocabulary.

Pur was a commonly established practice used among the people in the Old Testament times to determine the direction or solution in a given situation. In the Bible it is listed seventy times in the Old Testament and seven times in the New Testament.

However, in the New Testament you will not see this practice of *casting Pur* used by the Christians except one time. The one recorded occasion was when the disciples used it to cast lots to determine which of the two men among their group should be selected to replace Judas Iscariot (Acts 1:26).

You will not see Pur mentioned again *after* the arrival of the Holy Spirit as vividly described in the second chapter of Acts. The Holy Spirit has the divine assignment and responsibility as both Guide and Counselor for the Christian.

News of Haman's evil plan spread rapidly throughout the Jewish community. For several months the Jews were placed in deadly jeopardy knowing that on a set day they were to be killed. It was as though they were sitting on death row with an execution date only a few months away.

To insure his wicked scheme was implemented Haman approached the king.

> Then Haman said to King Ahasuerus, 'There is a certain people scattered and dispersed among the people in all the provinces of your kingdom; their laws are different from all other people's, and they do not keep the king's laws. Therefore, it is not fitting for the king to let them remain. If it pleases the king, let a decree be written that they be destroyed, and I will pay ten thousand talents of silver into the hands of those who do the work, to bring it into the king's treasuries.' So the king took his signet ring from his hand and gave it to Haman, the son of Hammedatha the Agagite, the enemy of the Jews. (Esther 3:8-10)

Notice that King Ahasuerus did not discuss nor ask any questions about this evil plan. How easy it was for the king to be fooled.

Here are the enticements Haman offered to the king to insure his wicked scheme would be approved:

1. Haman offered to pay money to all those who would carry out his dastardly deed.

2. Haman ordered all the spoils of the Jewish race be plundered and brought into the king's treasuries.

3. Since this *certain people* (the Jews) were not obeying the king's laws, Haman insinuated the Jews must be against the king and therefore these bad people must be annihilated.

4. It appeared to be a win-win for the Persian Empire and thus for the king.

We do not see any place where the king first checked into what Haman was telling him. He had already begun to trust Haman and he was allowing him to basically run the kingdom for him. With little or no thought and no moral conscience the king hands over his signet ring, his authority, to Haman.

I wonder how many of our rulers since King Ahasuerus have handed over their authority to Satan? They have given it away. They have relinquished their own authority, the people's lands and the people's money to the enemy—Satan.

With that surrender of authority Satan runs rampant attempting to destroy all the *certain Christians* that he can. He still has a *certain* people that he wants to destroy. Those *certain* people today are the ones that would follow wholeheartedly Jesus Christ.

In Esther 3:12 we are told that the king's scribes were called on the thirteenth day of the first month (the Gregorian calendar month of March or April) and a decree was written according to all that Haman commanded. "In the name of King Ahasuerus it was written, and sealed with the king's signet ring."

Looking back at the timeline we see that Haman's inner circle had cast Pur for the date of the execution of the Jews prior to Haman going in to speak to the king. Haman just needed to move one more piece of the puzzle in his direction for his plan to be complete. He needed the signet ring to issue the decree in the king's name.

Even with all Haman's authority as chief of all the rulers of the Persian lands, he still did not have the authority to write an unbreakable decree. Haman wanted this decree to be unbreakable. He wanted the king's signet ring. And he got it!

After Haman writes the decree and seals it with the king's signet ring, he sends the letters out all across the Persian empire. There is now a set date of execution. He implemented his evil plan and revenge is set in motion.

Haman can now sit down with the king and the two of them can have a drink together. I think the king believes he will be restoring peace to his kingdom. Haman believes he will be exacting revenge upon a *certain* people. Both celebrated, but for different reasons (Esther 3:13-15).

Esther 3:15: "But the city of Shushan was perplexed." The people of the capital were confused over what they saw. I do not believe this decree by Haman was entirely supported by all the people.

The people in the city of Shushan witnessed a divided leadership. The king appeared to have given away his authority and the chief ruler, Haman, appeared to have forgotten about the people of Persia—he was only interested in destroying a *certain* people.

I wonder how much we might see the same story playing out today within our own country? Just food for thought…

Here are some interesting reflective notes:

+ Chapter 1 ends with Queen Vashti deposed from the throne and decrees have been sent out all across the Persian empire concerning the role of the woman within the home and the language of the house.
+ Chapter 2 ended with the two king's doormen being hanged and the circumstances recorded in the book of the chronicles in the presence of the king.
+ Chapter 3 ends with the king and Haman celebrating for different reasons, and Shushan the citadel is in a state of perplexed apprehension.

These all appear to be very unfortunate or even tragic endings if this story was to conclude at this point. We will see what happens in the next chapter as this story continues to unfold.

Chapter 4

If I Perish, I Perish (473 BC)

Esther 4:1-3 begins with Mordecai hearing of the unbreakable decree from Haman that is being rapidly dispatched all across the kingdom. He quickly grasped the grave consequences intended for his people, the Jews. Grief burdened his soul as Mordecai mournfully clothed himself in sackcloth and ashes. With a broken heart he roamed the city crying bitterly and loudly.

Similar circumstances face our country today. Jesus is coming soon. Are our people ready? The harvest is white and the laborers are few (John 4:35). Who will go, and who will tell them to be prepared for the Lord's return?

Death is a part of life, but our final destination depends upon our choice while we are alive. As with the Jews in Mordecai's day, grave consequences face our people today without Christ. Do we share the same degree of burden for our generation today that possessed Mordecai for his people in his day?

Satan has not relented in his desire to kill and to destroy God's children. We, as God's children, must remain vigilant and prepared to sound the midnight cry before the return of Christ.

Continuing Mordecai's intense response to Haman's decree, we look at Esther 4:4: "So Esther's maids and eunuchs came and told her, and the queen was deeply distressed. Then she sent garments to clothe Mordecai and take his sackcloth away from him, but he would not accept them."

No one loved and cherished Mordecai more than Queen Esther. Her kind gestures to Mordecai were from her heart as she tried to console him. But the inconsolable Mordecai firmly dismissed her efforts to comfort him. He refused to stop his public mourning outside the gate of the king's court.

Do you think that Esther was attempting to get him back within the confines of the king's court so no matter what might happen outside the gates he would be safe? We can only surmise what thoughts Queen Esther had during this intense situation.

Esther could not understand what was going on in Mordecai's mind. Why has he refused to let go of his sackcloth? Anxiously she sends the king's eunuch, Hathach, to determine why Mordecai was so heavily grieved (Esther 4:5).

Mordecai verbally gives Hathach a brief history of Haman's evil plot to destroy the Jewish race. Mordecai prepares to dispatch Hathach back to Esther with a copy of Haman's decree approved by King Ahasuerus.

Just prior to dispatching Hathach, Mordecai instructs him to explain the evil decree to Esther. Then Mordecai insists that Hathach command Esther to go in to the king and make supplication to him and plead before him for her people. Esther 4:8 tells us that Hathach returns and follows explicitly all of the instructions from Mordecai.

In Esther 4:10-12 we find that Esther told Hathach to go back to Mordecai and remind him of the royal protocol for how one should approach the king (this included even the queen). She said to tell Mordecai that it had been thirty days since she had an audience with the king. In other words, she did not know when the king would call her again.

> And Mordecai told them to answer Esther: 'Do not think in your heart that you will escape in the king's palace any more than all the other Jews. For if you remain completely silent at this time, relief and deliverance will arise for the Jews from another place, but you and your father's house will perish. Yet who knows whether you have come to the kingdom for such a time as this?' (Esther 4:13-14)

That epic last phrase spoken by Mordecai pierced the heart and soul of Esther and opened her spiritual eyes to her destiny.

Mordecai had just challenged her to step into her destiny that would ultimately affect not only her Jewish people but all generations to follow. Esther embraced her destiny knowing she might face death for her bold and brave actions!

Just as Esther faced tough questions, we too must ask ourselves some difficult questions facing us today:

1. To what extent can a Christian hide in the world?
2. To what extent can a sinner hide within the church?
3. Is there a spiritual dilemma with a Christian trying to blend in and mingle with the world?
4. Is there a problem with a sinner trying to blend in to look like believers within the church?

A reasonable observation and conclusion is that both will be miserable. Eventually both are going to slip up and reveal their true identity. Each must make a decision at some point whether to continue to be a sinner or choose to be a Christian. Our choice will determine our destiny.

Mordecai sent back to Esther these words: "Relief and deliverance will arise for the Jews from another place." How would you interpret Mordecai's admonishment?

1. Is it possible for us to miss our assignment from God?
2. Is courage required to fulfill our assignment from the Lord?
3. Will God still fulfill His Word with or without us?
4. If we do not obey what God has told us to do, to what extent will it affect our current and succeeding generations?

One unequivocal response to these questions is that God will always carry out His plans. He has offered you a chance to be a part of His plan. You were born for a specific time and purpose in God's plan. God has a divine destiny for you!

We can ignore God's plan and miss our calling, but only through disobedience to His voice. Gather up spiritual courage and boldly step into your destiny with determination and conviction.

God has made provision for us to be properly equipped to fulfill God's purpose for our lives. Jesus told His disciples in Luke 24:49: "Behold, I send the Promise of My Father upon you; but tarry in the city of Jerusalem until you are endued with power from on high."

Being baptized in the Holy Spirit, which is the Promise of our Father, gives us the spiritual power we need to carry out His assignments with spiritual boldness.

God will still fulfill His Word with or without us. I choose to respond to His call "Here am I! Send me" (Isaiah 6:8). Just as Mordecai admonished Esther, if we are disobedient to God's plan for our lives it will affect not only our own lives, but also those of many generations to come.

We read in Esther 4:15-17 that Esther told Mordecai to go and tell the people closest to him (the people of Shushan) to begin to fast for her for three days and nights. Esther and her maids would do the same in her palace chambers.

It is essential that we earnestly pray for those who are assigned a mission from the Lord. Prayer and fasting are powerful tools ordained by God for spiritual warfare.

Let us briefly summarize events up to this point:

Chapter 1 ends with Queen Vashti deposed from her position as Queen, and decrees being sent out all across the Persian empire regulating the role of the woman within the home as well as the language of the house.

Chapter 2 ends with the story of Mordecai saving the life of the king being carefully recorded in the book of the chronicles.

Chapter 3 ends with the king and Haman celebrating (for different reasons) and the capital city of Shushan is in a state of perplexed apprehension.

Chapter 4 ends with a date of execution for the entire Jewish race, a determined Esther, and a call to fasting (praying).

Will the end of chapter 4 stimulate pivotal events necessary to overthrow Haman and all his schemes, or will this be the end of the Jewish race and all of God's promises to his people?

We must continue this story to discover the outcome.

⌒ Chapter 5 ⌒

If It Pleases the King (473 BC)

As previously discussed, chapter 4 ends with a date of execution for the entire Jewish race, a determined Esther, and a call to prayer and fasting.

+ The date of the execution of the Jews, Esther 3:13, was set for the thirteenth day of the twelfth month of Adar (Gregorian calendar dates of February-March).
+ A brave and bold Esther was determined to obey Mordecai and present herself to the king. And if she perishes, she perishes!
+ Esther had called for Mordecai and his people to begin three days of fasting (praying) for her, with Esther and her maids also fasting (and praying) in the palace.

Put yourself in Esther's place just for a moment so you can grasp a glimpse of her dilemma. Do I fast and pray, or go and stand before the king not knowing if I am going to live or die?

Are spiritual battles won in heavenly places? Is our battle fought with flesh and blood on this earth? If our battles are won in prayer, then why do we all too often stand before the world's king with the thought of death hanging over us? Esther understood that spiritual warfare would have to be fought before ever stepping into the king's palace courtyard to meet him (Ephesians 6:12).

Knowing the gravity of her assignment from Mordecai, Esther calls upon the Jewish people to begin fasting (praying) on her behalf. She was about to face a battle that she alone could not win. She needed God's intervention.

I believe God gives us two great examples of intercessory prayer in the New Testament to be used as models for us in today's time. Let us examine these examples of effective intercessory prayer. Both involved Jesus being the Intercessor for us.

Jesus intercedes for Peter...

> And the Lord said, 'Simon, Simon! Indeed, Satan has asked for you, that he may sift you as wheat. But I have prayed for you, that your faith should not fail; and when you have returned to Me, strengthen your brethren.' But he said to Him, 'Lord, I am ready to go with You, both to prison and to death.' Then He said, 'I tell you, Peter, the rooster shall not crow this day before you will deny three times that you know Me.' (Luke 22:31-34)

Jesus knew that Peter would grow weak in the face of adversity so Jesus interceded for him through prayer. Then Jesus told

Peter that he would be returning to Him. Jesus modeled the perfect example of intercessory prayer with a faith that spoke life to Peter's destiny.

Jesus intercedes for the world…

> And He was withdrawn from them about a stone's throw, and He knelt down and prayed, saying, 'Father, if it is Your will, take this cup away from Me; nevertheless not My will, but Yours, be done.' Then an angel appeared to Him from heaven, strengthening Him. And being in agony, He prayed more earnestly. Then His sweat became like great drops of blood falling down to the ground. When He rose up from prayer, and had come to His disciples, He found them sleeping from sorrow. (Luke 22:41-45)

In this second example a noteworthy observation must be pointed out. When the angel appeared to Jesus from heaven, and strengthened Him, the scripture does not say *then* Jesus walked back to His disciples to continue the conversation. No, once strengthened, He *returned to pray* even more earnestly!

Jesus was in a battle. The angel had come to Jesus and brought Him strength. I do not know the exact nature of that strength, but it was so critical that the angel gave it to Jesus to equip Him to successfully win the spiritual battle. He went back into prayer with such intensity that His sweat became like great drops of blood falling on the ground.

Prayer of intercession is not easy. Rest assured that God will strengthen you when you become weak if He has called you to prayer. Return to your prayer closet in His strength if you are deeply engaged in a spiritual battle that must be won.

> Then He came to His disciples and said to them, 'Are you still sleeping and resting? Behold, the hour is at hand, and the Son of Man is being betrayed into the hands of sinners. Rise, let us be going. See, My betrayer is at hand.' (Matthew 26:45-46)

I believe this is the question that Jesus would ask us today. Are you *still* sleeping and resting? Just as Jesus declared that the hour is at hand can we also recognize that our time is also at hand? Just as Jesus was being betrayed are not our people today also being betrayed and deceived?

Today Satan is alive and well drawing spiritually blind people into his web of deceit. Are we still sleeping and resting while the world is dying? Let us return to our prayer closets, our war rooms, and fight the good fight of faith until we know that we have won the battle in the name of Jesus.

The previous chapters have opened with a few years between each chapter. This time there is only a three-day time lapse between chapter 4 and chapter 5.

Changes occurred between time spans in the book of Esther. We also have experienced significant changes in our values during certain time spans in our own country.

Changes first started slowly with the removal of prayer from public schools. After several decades, prayer was removed from sporting events. Then just a little bit later the Bible was eliminated from schools and courts.

Now we find America in a tailspin with moral decay crumbling the core values of the foundation of our nation. Things are not happening one at a time any longer. Now they are coming in bunches all across this land. When we let Satan's toe in our nation's door he was then able to kick it wide open.

Back to the book of Esther, we see the clock is moving fast. The calendar pages are turning quickly and the day of the Jews' execution is rapidly approaching.

The future of the Jewish people looks very grim. There appears to be no hope and they seem utterly helpless. The Persian and Medes law cannot be changed. They are being sold out even to their neighbors who were accepting Haman's blood money.

To save the Jewish people from annihilation, Esther quickly developed a plan. Fasting by Esther and her people for three days was the first phase of this plan. The second phase included Esther preparing two banquets for the king and Haman.

During the three specified days of prayer and fasting Esther is still very active making arrangements for confronting the enemy. She is preparing the banquet for the king and Haman (the enemy of the Jews). What courage she displays!

It takes courage to take action in your determination to obey. It is one thing to bow our knees and pray and even to fast a meal on behalf of ourselves or others. But it is an entirely different matter to carry out the command of the Lord that could most likely end in our death. That commitment requires tremendous moral and spiritual strength that only God can provide.

Moving forward, the opening scene in chapter 5 finds Queen Esther determined to get an audience with King Ahasuerus.

"Now it happened on the third day that Esther put on her royal robes and stood in the inner court of the king's palace, across from the king's house, while the king sat on his royal throne in the royal house, facing the entrance of the house." (Esther 5:1)

We see in Esther 5:2 that the king holds out the golden scepter to Esther which is the royal signal to safely approach the king. It is my guess this is the first good breath Esther has breathed in the last three days.

In Esther 5:3 the king asked Esther if she had a wish or request as he had not called for her. King Ahasuerus knew the law and he recognized Queen Esther had just risked her life to approach him. Esther must have been extremely relieved when the king told her that he would grant her request up to half of his kingdom.

Esther was very wise in allowing time for her plan to unfold. It would have been easy for her to just say "make this enemy of the Jews go away!" But such a hasty and flippant request may not have been favorably considered by the king.

Queen Esther understood this delicate situation and presented a request that appealed to the king. In Esther 5:4 she tells the king, "If it pleases the king, let the king and Haman come today to the banquet that I have prepared for him."

Have you noticed how our time is most often *not* the same as God's time? Esther had been working for three days preparing a banquet for the king and Haman, and she had a second banquet being prepared even while they were speaking to one another.

The scheduling of two separate banquets was not incidental. God had something critical to do that night between the banquets. God needed one more day to create the atmosphere for Esther to receive the destined answer from the king.

Her patience in asking the king to come twice to her home was from the Lord. The king asked Esther, "What is your petition?" (Esther 5:6). "Let the king and Haman come to the banquet which I will prepare for them, and tomorrow I will do as the king has said." (Esther 5:8)

Haman leaves the first banquet feeling good about himself and filled with self-righteousness. He thought he had just been honored and certainly he was basking in his own glory and honor.

Proverbs 16:18 says, "Pride goes before destruction, and a haughty spirit before a fall." And Proverbs 16:5 reads, "Everyone proud in heart is an abomination to the Lord; though they join forces, none will go unpunished."

"But when Haman saw Mordecai in the king's gate, and that he did not stand or tremble before him, he was filled with indignation against Mordecai." (Esther 5:9) Haman's hatred of Mordecai was so strong that it quickly crushed any joy he may have relished at the banquet.

Hatred and bitterness can quickly tarnish everything good in our lives. We soon forget how blessed we may have been. We are blind to our blessings and only focus on the target of our hatred and bitterness.

Esther 5:10-13 tells us that Haman calls his friends and his wife, Zeresh. He brags about his wealth and his many great accomplishments. But due to his hatred and bitterness he openly expresses, "Yet all this avails me nothing, so long as I see Mordecai the Jew sitting at the king's gate" (Esther 5:13).

Bitterness! Hatred! Ugliness! These conditions of the heart are like terminal cancer to our soul.

In Esther 5:14 we learn that Haman's wife, Zeresh, and his friends all suggest that he construct a seventy-five-foot high gallows and hang Mordecai in the morning *before* he goes to his personal invitation to the queen's banquet with the king.

Haman jumped at this suggestion and ordered the gallows to be built immediately. This hasty decision reflected his wicked heart as well as his poor choice of friends and counselors.

Chapter 5 ends with the hammering of the gallows echoing through the night. It had not been announced within the city who was to be hung.

Notwithstanding, the hammering of the gallows could not have gone unnoticed. The repetitive sound was music to Haman's ears through the night. In his mind he was about to begin his revenge!

Chapter 6

The Long, Long Night (473 BC)

The Long, Long Night....

"That night the king could not sleep. So one was commanded to bring the book of the records of the chronicles; and they were read before the king." (Esther 6:1)

The story that was read that night to the king was the documentation of Mordecai overhearing the plot of two of the king's doorkeepers to kill the king. Mordecai relayed this plot to Queen Esther who then informed King Ahasuerus. This report of Mordecai saving the king's life had actually been placed into the book of the chronicles about five years earlier.

Why was that story chosen on that particular night? Just think how many weeks or months or even longer would have to transpire before that particular passage about Mordecai would have been read to the king. That, my friend, is divine destiny!

When we read the book of Esther, unless we have studied it thoroughly and paid careful attention to each detail, we will most likely not notice this detail or assign significance to it. Casual reading of the scriptures can cause us to miss the real meat of the Word.

Was the one who was commanded to bring the book that night aware of the talk in the town concerning what was about to happen to Mordecai? Did he pick a *certain* story to read to the king? I doubt it.

Regardless of how it happened, I believe it was *not* an accident or a coincidence that this one specific story was read to the king *that* night. And just how often did the king have sleepless nights? I cannot help but wonder if it was the hammering of the gallows through the night that had kept him awake.

The king asked in Esther 6:3: "What honor or dignity has been bestowed on Mordecai for this? And the king's servant who attended him said, 'Nothing has been done for him.'"

The conversation ends between the servant and the king with no action taken at that moment. But the seed had been planted that night into the king's heart to give birth and bring to light an unfinished piece of history.

So often we feel as though nothing was done for us when it should have been done. We think we are forgotten and alone. But frequently God reserves a blessing for a later date in order to use it to our fullest advantage. This is exactly what we see happening here with the king and Mordecai. God is never late in His divine timing.

The Next Morning

As we observe in Esther 6:4-5, Haman was up bright and early the next morning to scurry to the king's outer court. Haman had probably listened to the hammering of the gallows throughout the night and more than likely did not sleep well.

This was his big moment. He was going to the palace to plant in the king's mind the thought to get rid of that rebellious Mordecai once and for all. Haman was thinking that since in only a few months he would be getting rid of all the Jews, he might as well get rid of Mordecai now.

Haman calculated the king would think his plan was magnificent. He was standing in the king's court anxiously anticipating an invitation into the king's presence. Haman was eager to share how he had already built gallows to hang Mordecai.

There was another time when Haman initiated action prior to obtaining the king's blessings. You will remember that Haman had already cast Pur for the date of execution *before* he had gotten the king's permission to execute the entire Jewish race. Here we see Haman up to his same old tricks again which was acting *before* permission from the king had been granted.

Satan can make deceitful and evil plans much like Haman did concerning Mordecai. But just as Haman had no authority, Satan has *no* authority to act upon his plans. God has final authority!

Haman is certainly no different than any other of the characters of the Bible, or of today's political times either. Haman's existence, as we have learned from history by reading in 1 Samuel 15, was the result of a disobedient act by King Saul. Haman would have never been born if Saul had obeyed God from the beginning. We clearly see how present and future generations may suffer grave consequences when we fail to completely obey God's directions.

Continuing the story, we find that Haman is welcomed into the king's presence and is about to be asked an important question.

Recall the king had just gone through a sleepless night and had asked for the book of the chronicles to be read to him. The king was lying in bed pondering what to do to honor the hero, Mordecai. He certainly had a completely different agenda on his mind than that of Haman that morning.

"So Haman came in, and the king asked him, 'What shall be done for the man whom the king delights to honor?' Now Haman thought in his heart, 'Whom would the king delight to honor more than me?'" (Esther 6:6)

Keeping this verse in mind, I will digress a moment and look at another prideful figure we see in the Bible. Lucifer, also called Satan, was the epitome of pride. See if you can find a likeness to Haman in these next few verses.

> How you are fallen from heaven, O Lucifer, son of
> the morning! How you are cut down to the ground,

you who weakened the nations! For you have said
in your heart: 'I will ascend into heaven, I will exalt
my throne above the stars of God; I will also sit on
the mount of the congregation on the farthest sides
of the north; I will ascend above the heights of the
clouds, I will be like the Most High.' Yet you shall
be brought down to Sheol, to the lowest depths of
the Pit. (Isaiah 14:12-15)

So, with a prideful spirit, and convinced that the king is
referring to himself as the one the king wants to honor, Haman
answers the king's question.

Let a royal robe be brought which the king has worn,
and a horse on which the king has ridden, which has
a royal crest placed on its head. Then let this robe
and horse be delivered to the hand of one of the
king's most noble princes, that he may array the man
whom the king delights to honor. Then parade him
on horseback through the city square, and proclaim
before him: 'Thus shall it be done to the man whom
the king delights to honor!' (Esther 6:8-9)

Observe the similarities between Haman and Lucifer. Both
have this elite perception of themselves as if they were the
chosen ones. They promoted themselves to the highest position
above all others. Each asserted himself to be like the King.

Back to the story in Esther 6:10: "Then the king said to
Haman, 'Hurry, take the robe and the horse, as you have
suggested, and do so for Mordecai the Jew who sits within

the king's gate! Leave nothing undone of all that you have spoken.'"

Please allow me to digress once again. I recall another time and place when the righteous Son of God was ushered into the city of Jerusalem riding upon a donkey. Throwing their robes on the ground, the excited crowd enthusiastically welcomed Jesus with fervent shouts of praise.

All this was done that it might be fulfilled which was spoken by the prophet, saying:

> Tell the daughter of Zion, 'Behold, your King is coming to you, lowly, and sitting on a donkey, a colt, the foal of a donkey.' So the disciples went and did as Jesus commanded them. They brought the donkey and the colt, laid their clothes on them, and set Him on them. And a very great multitude spread their clothes on the road; others cut down branches from the trees and spread them on the road. Then the multitudes who went before and those who followed cried out, saying:

> 'Hosanna to the Son of David! 'Blessed is He who comes in the name of the LORD!' Hosanna in the highest!'

> And when He had come into Jerusalem, all the city was moved, saying, 'Who is this?'

> So the multitudes said, 'This is Jesus, the prophet from Nazareth of Galilee.' (Matthew 21:4-11)

This triumphant entry of Jesus into Jerusalem with the crowds celebrating his arrival must have enraged Lucifer (Satan). To witness all the unsolicited praise and adoration of the people toward Jesus created unbearable envy in Lucifer. He would have halted the parade if he could. But Satan had no power then and he has no power now.

Before we examine Haman's reaction to the king's command to honor Mordecai the Jew in Esther 6:10, we must recall Esther 3:8: "Then Haman said to King Ahasuerus, 'There is a *certain people* scattered and dispersed among your kingdom....'"

Haman deceptively omitted any reference to the Jewish race when he suggested his evil plan to the king. He proposed to destroy only *a certain people* who were different from all other people and were not obeying the king's laws.

In today's society we label those who disobey the law as "criminals". So Haman's scheme involved bringing these criminals, or a *certain people,* to justice on the set day (as calculated by Pur). He deceived the king into believing the decree would eliminate all the criminals so the kingdom could be peaceful.

It is my conviction that the king did not know that these criminals identified by Haman were actually the Jewish people. If King Ahasuerus had known these criminals were Jews, then he would not have selected Mordecai the Jew to be honored.

It was no secret to the king that Mordecai was a Jew. Mordecai had not hidden his race from the king, nor from the community. Mordecai had only instructed Queen Esther that she was to keep silent concerning her heritage.

What a shock it must have been to Haman when the king ordered him to "take the robe and the horse, as you [Haman] have suggested, and do so for Mordecai the Jew who sits within the king's gate!" (Esther 6:10).

It certainly appears Haman's selfish and evil plan completely backfired! By attempting to deceive the king by not mentioning the Jewish people by name he unwittingly opened the door for the king to select a Jew to honor.

To further shame and humiliate Haman the king selected the one Jew that Haman so bitterly hated, Mordecai. Since the king approved his suggestion, Haman had no option other than to fulfill his own recommendation by honoring Mordecai.

Now a very humiliated, angry, anxious, and helpless Haman carries out the king's order to honor Mordecai. With his dignity stripped, Haman leads Mordecai around the city and proclaims Mordecai as the one the king delights to honor.

After this parade Haman hurries home with his head covered. In a matter of minutes, he had tumbled from the highest expectations of honor to the lowest pits of humiliation (Esther 6:11-12).

To add to Haman's perilous predicament, his wife Zeresh and his wise men distance themselves from Haman. They see the writing on the wall that Haman's life is the one now in grave danger, not Mordecai, and they want no part of it (Esther 6:13).

While they were still talking with Haman, the king's eunuchs came, and hastened to bring Haman to the banquet which Esther had prepared for them. This intriguing scene closes chapter 6 (Esther 6:14).

Just one long, long night can make a monumental difference in our lives when we trust God. Mordecai trusted God and his obedience impacted the world eternally.

Timelines are important, and critically so is God's timeline. Esther, chapter 1, begins in the third year of King Ahasuerus's reign. We are now in the twelfth year of the king's reign. Although these six chapters span nine years, chapters five and six transpire in three days.

God's concept of time is totally different than ours. God is always active on our behalf. However, we may not always see all the pieces of the mosaic of our life. Each detail in God's plan occurs in a certain order and in His perfect time. That leaves us with only one choice: we must trust Him.

Please take notice that just as the timeline in the book of Esther is racing towards Haman's own demise, God's timeline in the New Testament warns us that the time is rapidly approaching for His return for His children. Satan will very soon be exposed as a liar and thief. Revelation is just around the corner.

"The devil, who deceived them, was cast into the lake of fire and brimstone where the beast and the false prophet are. And they will be tormented day and night forever and ever." (Revelation 20:10)

─᠃ *Chapter 7* ᠃─

Haman is Hanged (473 BC)

Chapter 6 ends with prophetic words spoken to Haman by his wife, Zeresh. "If Mordecai, before whom you have begun to fall, is of Jewish descent, you will not prevail against him but will surely fall before him." (Esther 6:13)

Such prophetic words spoken by Zeresh that day! Little did she know she was comparing her husband Haman to Satan. Her words still ring true today.

Look at the reference in this scripture "…is of Jewish descent." Who else is of Jewish descent against whom the world will not prevail? We clearly see parallels between Mordecai and Haman that represent the spiritual battle today between Jesus Christ and Satan.

Chapter 7 begins with the king and Haman quickly rushing off to the second banquet that Esther had prepared for them for the next day. Esther had their undivided attention. This second banquet was quite different from the first (Esther 7:1-2).

The first banquet had been so delightful and entertaining that the king wanted to come back and continue the festivities. Queen Esther knew how to throw a banquet for the king. She was keenly aware of his tastes and understood what appealed to his sense of pleasure.

Once again Queen Esther found favor in his sight so the king for the second time asked her what request he could grant. This time she shocks him with the following perplexing revelation:

> Then Queen Esther answered and said, 'If I have found favor in your sight, O king, and if it pleases the king, let my life be given me at my petition, and my people at my request. For we have been sold, my people and I, to be destroyed, to be killed, and to be annihilated. Had we been sold as male and female slaves, I would have held my tongue, although the enemy could never compensate for the king's loss.' (Esther 7:3-4)

What? The king is totally shocked and perplexed with this request! Is he about to lose his dearly beloved Queen Esther? Is she about to lose her life, and her own people as well? Who is this evil traitor? How could this take place in his own secure palace? All these thoughts are racing through his enraged mind.

Esther had just informed the king of this evil plot that was unfolding right under his nose without his knowledge. The wrath of King Ahasuerus arose quickly as he demanded that this traitor's identity be revealed.

Since Haman represents the spirit of Satan, this situation described by Esther should remind us of what Jesus warned in John 10:10: "The thief does not come except to steal, and to kill, and to destroy."

The king can no longer hold his tongue. He demands immediate answers to his questions. Where is this thief? Where is this traitor?

> So King Ahasuerus answered and said to Queen Esther, 'Who is he, and where is he, who would dare presume in his heart to do such a thing?' And Esther said, 'The adversary and enemy is this wicked Haman!' So Haman was terrified before the king and queen. (Esther 7:5-6)

This scripture captures one of the key teaching points of this book. Please take careful notice that Haman is terrified before the king and the queen. Drawing a parallel, it could be said that Satan is terrified before God and the bride of Christ. The bride of Christ refers to born again believers.

The book of Esther clearly demonstrates that evil can be directly attributed to Satan and righteousness can be directly attributed to God the Father, God the Son (Jesus), and God the Holy Spirit. These three in one comprise the Holy Trinity.

Did you observe the intense anger that quickly arose in the bosom of King Ahasuerus when he learned someone would dare harm his bride? That scene in the palace is a picture of

God and His intimate relationship with the bride of Christ. God will do whatever it takes to protect His bride.

So often we get it all backwards. We act as though we, the bride of Christ, are the ones on the run. No, take a firm stand! Put on the whole armor of God as found in Ephesians 6:10-18.

Satan can only stay in areas that we give him permission. He owns no part of this earth or your life. Even the earth quaked at the death and resurrection of Jesus Christ.

> And Jesus cried out again with a loud voice, and yielded up His spirit. Then, behold, the veil of the temple was torn in two from top to bottom; and the earth quaked, and the rocks were split. (Matthew 27:50-51)

The earth does not want the presence of Satan any more than we do. Cast Satan out of your life and family with the authority you have as the bride of Christ. Satan is terrified of you as the bride of Christ, the queen of the Almighty King.

All too often we do not assume our rightful position as queen or the bride of Christ. We remain in our pre-salvation position as pauper. We act as though we were still living outside the palace.

Just as Queen Esther was moved into the palace when she married the king, we too are moved into the kingdom of God when we become the bride of Christ. We have the entire army of God at our right hand if we really grasp our royal position.

Continuing the scene in the palace:

> Then the king arose in his wrath from the banquet
> of wine and went into the palace garden; but
> Haman stood before Queen Esther, pleading for
> his life, for he saw that evil was determined against
> him by the king. When the king returned from the
> palace garden to the place of the banquet of wine,
> Haman had fallen across the couch where Esther
> was. Then the king said, 'Will he also assault
> the queen while I am in the house?' As the word
> left the king's mouth, they covered Haman's face.
> (Esther 7:7-8)

Please pay close attention to what is transpiring in this scene. Haman is pleading with Esther for his life. Does that sound like a strong man to you? Do you see that this weak and terrified Haman is finally exposed? We should be exposing Satan as weak and terrified just like Esther saw Haman.

Take notice that the king states once again something very prophetic that we need to hear as the bride of Christ. He asks if Haman will also assault the queen while the king is in the house.

Can Satan bring harm to the bride of Christ as long as the King is *in the house?* Where is His *house* today? Are we not the temple of the Lord? Is Christ living within your bodily temple this moment?

61

1 Corinthians 6:19-20 says, "Or do you not know that your body is the temple of the Holy Spirit who is in you, whom you have from God, and you are not your own? For you were bought at a price; therefore glorify God in your body and in your spirit, which are God's."

Satan cannot harm you as long as the King is in the house. Does that mean we will never have tests or adverse situations? Absolutely not! We see that Haman fell across the couch where Esther sat and it gave an appearance of her being assaulted. She was not actually assaulted. The king and his servants were still in the house; she was never in harm's way.

King David declared, "Yea, though I walk through the valley of the shadow of death, I will fear no evil; for You are with me; Your rod and Your staff, they comfort me." (Psalm 23:4)

In Psalm 23:6, he continues by declaring, "Surely goodness and mercy shall follow me all the days of my life, and I will dwell in the house of the Lord forever."

King David spoke of an *appearance of death*. A shadow is only an appearance, a resemblance of something. It is not the real thing. A thought to ponder is that a shadow occurs only in the presence of light. And Jesus is The Light!

Also notice as long as we dwell within the house of the Lord (remain His child), He will assign two "angels", Goodness and Mercy, to follow us all the days of our lives.

What a comforting promise! Although I have heard goodness and mercy referred to as character traits, I love the thought of them being two angels. You decide. We win either way!

Now back to our story.

> Now Harbonah, one of the eunuchs, said to the king, 'Look! The gallows, fifty cubits high, which Haman made for Mordecai, who spoke good on the king's behalf, is standing at the house of Haman.' Then the king said, 'Hang him on it!' So they hanged Haman on the gallows that he had prepared for Mordecai. Then the king's wrath subsided. (Esther 7:9-10)

Vengeance was not exacted at the hand of Queen Esther or Mordecai. Their personal role in the consequences facing Haman was limited to reporting what they heard and knew to the king. In fact, Harbonah, one of the king's eunuchs, points out the gallows to the king which Haman had ordered to be built to hang Mordecai.

Paul tells us in Romans 12:19: "Beloved, do not avenge yourselves, but rather give place to wrath; for it is written, 'Vengeance is Mine, I will repay,' says the Lord."

Do you see how sinister this story would have been had Esther or Mordecai taken matters within their own hands? They probably would have lost everything. But when the king takes care of it, the outcome is entirely different. Jesus Christ, our

King, has the position as well as the authority to impose righteous justice.

We end chapter 7 in the book of Esther with Haman's head covered and Haman being escorted to the gallows. You might conclude that the story would end here. But at this point Esther, Mordecai, and the entire Jewish race are still in grave danger of being annihilated.

—☙ *Chapter 8* ❧—

The King's Decree and the Signet Ring (473 BC)

Chapter 7 dramatically ended with the king ordering Haman to be hanged on the gallows Haman had prepared for Mordecai. But Haman's death did not revoke the earlier decree sent out in the name of King Ahasuerus that the Jews were to be killed.

> And the letters were sent by couriers into all the king's provinces, to destroy, to kill, and to annihilate all the Jews, both young and old, little children and women, in one day, on the thirteenth day of the twelfth month, which is the month of Adar, and to plunder their possessions. (Esther 3:13)

This decree was written as an irrevocable decree according to the law of the Medes and Persians. Hanging Haman did not revoke this law nor prevent it from being enforced on the date set to begin the massacre of the Jewish people.

But God softened the heart of the king after his wrath subsided and he granted favor to Esther and Mordecai. "On that day

King Ahasuerus gave Queen Esther the house of Haman, the enemy of the Jews. And Mordecai came before the king, for Esther had told how he was related to her." (Esther 8:1)

Now look at Acts 16:31: "So they said, 'Believe on the Lord Jesus Christ, and you will be saved, you and your household.'" This verse assures us still today that those who are of our household are to be saved through believing on the Lord Jesus Christ as our Savior.

With the same confidence that we can approach our Savior and Lord today, Mordecai came before King Ahasuerus. Mordecai still had to give his allegiance to the king. But once he made that pledge, Mordecai was considered a part of the royal household of the king.

The king made this new relationship clear in Esther 8:2: "So the king took off his signet ring, which he had taken from Haman, and gave it to Mordecai; and Esther appointed Mordecai over the house of Haman." More will be said on this powerful verse a little later.

With the inevitable date of the annihilation of her people rapidly approaching, Queen Esther made the bold and brave decision to seek an audience with the king.

> Now Esther spoke once again to the king, fell down at his feet, and implored him with tears to counteract the evil of Haman the Agagite, and the scheme which he had devised against the Jews. And

> the king held out the golden scepter toward Esther. So Esther arose and stood before the king, and said, 'If it pleases the king, and if I have found favor in his sight and the thing seems right to the king and I am pleasing in his eyes, let it be written to revoke the letters devised by Haman, the son of Hammedatha the Agagite, which he wrote to annihilate the Jews who are in all the king's provinces. For how can I endure to see the evil that will come to my people? Or how can I endure to see the destruction of my countrymen? (Esther 8:3-6)

There is a divine order in Queen Esther's requests to King Ahasuerus. She first pleaded for the safety of her own life. Esther then urged the king to spare the life of her family, Mordecai. This was quickly followed by her request to save her people, the Jews.

In chapter 7, Esther first told the king she was about to be killed. She quickly recognized that in her birth status as a Jew her own life was in jeopardy as well as the life of Mordecai. Please take careful note that Esther sought help directly from the king who had the authority to save her, Mordecai, and her people.

Is not God, our King, still the only One today with the authority to save us when we are in spiritual danger? Are you praying for your own salvation? Are you approaching the throne of God to intercede on behalf of your unsaved family members?

Next, in chapter 8, Esther pleads her case to the king and describes the plight of her people to him. This time Esther is passionately advocating for the survival of the entire Jewish race, her countrymen.

Like Esther, are we praying passionately for the people that are lost in this world today? Do we possess the compassion that Jesus has for people that are headed to an eternity facing a burning hell where there will be weeping and gnashing of teeth?

> But He will say, 'I tell you I do not know you, where you are from. Depart from Me, all you workers of iniquity.' There will be weeping and gnashing of teeth, when you see Abraham and Isaac and Jacob and all the prophets in the kingdom of God, and yourselves thrust out. (Luke 13:27-28)

The Bible says Esther fell at the king's feet with tears flowing from her eyes for her people. She did not know them all by name, but she *knew their destiny*. They were a doomed race! She had to do everything that she could to petition the king for their lives.

We do not know all the people of the world by name, but we know their destiny if we cannot bring them into the household of God. We must be interceding on their behalf!

"Then King Ahasuerus said to Queen Esther and Mordecai the Jew, 'Indeed, I have given Esther the house of Haman, and they have hanged him on the gallows because he tried to lay his hand on the Jews.'" (Esther 8:7)

The king gave Esther the house of Haman. Who owns the house now? It is Esther, not Haman. Why do some children of The King allow Satan to remain and hang around the house when he no longer owns the house?

When Satan tries to enter your home, bar him from stepping foot into your royal home. He is trespassing! He has no right, nor authority, to enter your home. You are the temple of the Lord.

"You yourselves write a decree concerning the Jews, as you please, in the king's name, and seal it with the king's signet ring; for whatever is written in the king's name and sealed with the king's signet ring no one can revoke." (Esther 8:8)

As referenced earlier in Esther 8:2 and now Esther 8:8, this powerful verse births an immense revelation from the book of Esther. It is this:

You have already been given the King's signet ring, His name, and His authority!

It was several years ago that the Lord unfolded this powerful revelation to me after having read this story of Esther. I was standing in my kitchen canning some of my fruit from our property. I usually had no problem at all getting my jars to seal, but for some reason *not one* of the jars of this particular batch had sealed. Not one!

This had never before happened to me in the canning process. I read the canning booklet on what to do when the jars would not seal properly. The booklet's instructions said to wait until the next day and place the jars back into the water bath and repeat the whole process again to get them to seal properly.

It was now the next day and I had just completed the process the second time. Once again, not one jar sealed! I had even used brand new seals. I was totally stumped.

But that very morning I had been reading Esther, chapter 8, concerning the story of the king telling Esther that she now possessed the king's signet ring and "whatever is sealed with the king's signet ring no one can revoke" (Esther 8:8).

The entire revelation of what I was reading was coming alive to me at that very moment as I stood there in front of the unsealed jars. I prayed what I had understood from the scriptures:

> Lord, if I understand You correctly, we have been given authority to use Your name for the power and authority to combat the evilness of Satan. You have handed us the King's Signet Ring—the Seal—the Holy Spirit. Lord, if I have understood this correctly, would You do something for me? Would You seal these jars as I hold my own hand with my ring that is on my finger over each jar?

I stood and held my hand bearing my own ring, as though it were the King's Signet Ring, over the lid of the first jar. I decreed, "In the name of Jesus *be sealed!*"

All those who have done any canning know there is a popping sound that comes from the jar when the lid physically responds to the vacuum which is sealing the lid to the rim of the glass jar. I always called it music to my ears when I heard that popping sound as it confirmed the lids were sealed.

Sure enough, POP! I moved my ring finger over the next jar and repeated the same...POP! I continued this decree for all seven (that's right...seven!) jars that had previously refused to seal. All seven jars experienced a POP and all seven jars were sealed.

To make sure that God received all the glory from this miracle, not one jar sealed in advance of me decreeing it to seal. They sealed as I held my ring finger, exemplifying the Signet Ring of the Holy Spirit, over each jar one at a time.

God had confirmed something in my spirit that day. He had demonstrated to me visually the assurance that He had already given me everything that I needed to defeat the enemy.

There was not another person in my home at the time of this profound meeting with God. I was not trying to impress anyone with His miraculous power. I was trying to confirm something that He was showing *me* that day. Something that was about to push me forward in the Kingdom for Him.

Please take exceptional notice of the following phrase from verse eight that might change your concept of spiritual authority.

Esther 8:8: "You yourselves write a decree." So often we go to God and expect Him to fight the battle for us while we sit back and watch. But there are certain times when God wants us to proclaim our own decree against Satan.

God patiently, yet earnestly, wants us to understand that He has already given His children the Seal—The Holy Spirit. We can write (speak) a decree against the forces of Satan that can stop him dead in his tracks. But our words are powerless unless they are decreed with the seal of the Holy Spirit.

To better understand this authority God has provided, let us examine some New Testament verses concerning the Holy Spirit as our Seal.

> Now He who establishes us with you in Christ and anointed us is God, who also has sealed us and given us the Spirit in our hearts as a guarantee. (2 Corinthians 1:21-22)

> In Him you also trusted, after you heard the word of truth, the gospel of your salvation; in whom also, having believed, you were sealed with the Holy Spirit of promise, who is the guarantee of our inheritance until the redemption of the purchased possession, to the praise of His glory. (Ephesians 1:13-14)

> And do not grieve the Holy Spirit of God, by whom you were sealed for the day of redemption. (Ephesians 4:30)

Throughout history royal seals were used to identify and transfer significant documents and decrees. The royal seal guaranteed the authenticity of the document until the moment it was authorized to be revealed.

These referenced scriptures reveal the strong emphasis God places on His royal children being sealed by the Holy Spirit. God imprints the seal of the Holy Spirit upon us to demonstrate His guarantee of our inheritance until the day of redemption.

Mordecai understood the significance of his decree being sealed with the king's signet ring as seen in the following passage.

> So the king's scribes were called at that time, in the third month, which is the month of Sivan [May-June, Gregorian calendar], on the twenty-third day; and it was written, according to all that Mordecai commanded, to the Jews, the satraps, the governors, and the princes of the provinces from India to Ethiopia, one hundred and twenty-seven provinces in all, to every province in its own script, to every people in their own language, and to the Jews in their own script and language. And he wrote in the name of King Ahasuerus, sealed it with the king's signet ring, and sent letters by couriers on horseback, riding on royal horses bred from swift steeds. (Esther 8:9-10)

Notice that the king's scribes documented all that Mordecai commanded in the name of King Ahasuerus. Scribes were the trusted servants of the king. They faithfully recorded the spoken words of the king.

The writers of each book in the Bible are the spiritual scribes of all that is spoken by God the King. Through the inspiration of the Holy Spirit, each writer or scribe faithfully recorded exactly what God spoke to them. Through this God-ordained process the spoken Word became the written Word, which is the Bible.

All the words spoken by God and recorded in the Bible are for our benefit. The apostle Paul wrote the following passage.

> All Scripture is given by inspiration of God, and is profitable for doctrine, for reproof, for correction, for instruction in righteousness. (2 Timothy 3:16)

Mordecai's decree, written and sealed in the name of the king, was sent promptly to everyone in the kingdom. The letters were written in the language of each region so all could clearly understand the decree. The same people that had received Haman's letters, written in their own language, were now receiving the new decree that superseded Haman's letters.

We can take Mordecai's response to illustrate what God has done for us in revealing His spoken Word through the Bible. Mordecai insured no one was left out in being able to hear the decree. The royal letters were promptly hand-delivered by couriers who rode on royal horses bred for their swiftness.

So often we think God is not responding to our prayers or needs. We may think He is taking too long to answer us. We want Him to come to our rescue immediately. Be patient! The couriers are carrying your letters of freedom from destruction by the enemy on the King's swiftest horses. Psalm 147:15 says, "He sends out His command to the earth; His word runs very swiftly."

The letters written by Esther and Mordecai were different from Haman's letters. Haman had tried to buy the annihilation of the Jews with his own blood money. Haman boasted he would give the spoil of the Jews to the king. Perhaps he thought this offer would be an incentive to lure the king to sign this decree against the Jews.

Once again we look at the timeline of events. In Esther 3:7 we discover that in the first month, which is the month of Nisan (April), Haman and his men cast Pur for the date of destruction of the entire Jewish race. Esther 3:12 indicates Haman's decree was written and sent out on the thirteenth day of the first month.

Then look at when the letters from Esther and Mordecai were written in Esther 8:9: "so the king's scribes were called at that time, in the third month, which is the month of Sivan [late May or early June] on the twenty-third day."

It appears as though Haman's letters to annihilate the Jews for a price had at least a two month's head start on Esther's and Mordecai's letters. The significant difference was their letters to the Jews, God's people, now had the king's authority to overpower, destroy, and to kill all the evil forces that were deployed by Haman.

> By these letters the king permitted the Jews who were in every city to gather together and protect their lives—to destroy, kill, and annihilate all the forces of any people or province that would assault them, both little children and women, and to plunder their possessions, on one day in all the provinces of King Ahasuerus, on the thirteenth day of the twelfth month, which is the month of Adar. A copy of the document was to be issued as a decree in every province and published for all people, so that the Jews would be ready on that day to avenge themselves on their enemies. (Esther 8:11-13)

They were not directed to go out and destroy, harm, or in any way hurt their non-Jewish neighbors indiscriminately. The king permitted the Jews to only destroy those that would try to harm them. The Jewish people were authorized all the power they needed to protect themselves.

Please make special note in your Bible in Esther 8:11: "and to plunder their possessions." We will investigate that command in more detail a little later.

As stated earlier, Haman has a head start in implementing the death sentence against the Jews. His letter was dispatched in Nisan (April) and the date of execution of the Jews is the twelfth month, which is Adar (February-March). Mordecai's and Esther's letters were not transmitted until the month of Sivan (late May or early June).

What is amazing is both letters have the same effective date of implementing the decrees! Both were decreed to be effective on the thirteenth day of the twelfth month, which is Adar.

While both decrees have the same effective date, each decree carries a completely opposing message. Driven by hatred and bitterness, Haman's decree speaks of death and destruction and conveys no hope to the recipient.

Driven by divine purpose, Esther and Mordecai issue a decree that speaks of life, protection, and freedom from oppression for the Jewish people. Their decree reflected the desires of the king.

These two opposing attitudes of the heart are presented in Proverbs 18:21: "Death and life are in the power of the tongue, and those who love it will eat its fruit." Are you speaking death, or are you speaking life?

If you or a family member receive a bad report, regardless of the magnitude, God is aware of the situation before it even occurs. God is involved in the process of resolving your predicament so that His divine will is accomplished.

Take heart and refuge in the Word of God, whether spoken or written. When God decrees His response, rest assured it will come to pass just as He promises, and in His time.

What would have happened if the Jews had refused to listen to the second letter that was dispatched by Esther and Mordecai? They would have stood there helpless, blinded by fear and despair. Surrendering their rightful position to the enemy, their lack of faith would have rendered them powerless and hopeless.

Does that sound like some people today? I wonder how many have not heard the second letter, the letter of promise and of hope? How many may have heard but have refused to accept the second letter, the New Testament of Jesus Christ?

Like the couriers riding on the swift steeds in Esther, we must with the same sense of urgency dispatch the Word to every people in their own script and language. With time elapsing, we are commissioned to deliver to all the world the second letter.

If the listener heeds the second letter, they will inherit eternal life through Jesus Christ who is the Word. The second letter decrees the mercy and grace of God towards all mankind.

John 3:17 tells us, "For God did not send His Son into the world to condemn the world, but that the world through Him might be saved." The second letter is one filled with mercy and love.

However, if we refuse to believe the second letter (salvation), then we will die in our hopeless state. What a tragic and completely avoidable ending to a life that was created with a hope and a future designed and destined by God (Jeremiah 29:11).

As the story of the second decree continues we observe that the couriers hasten to deliver the king's command in Esther 8:14: "The couriers who rode on royal horses went out, hastened and pressed on by the king's command. And the decree was issued in Shushan the citadel."

As I read this verse, I am reminded of another significant moment in history that generated quite a dramatic response. My mind quickly jumps to the day of the Cross, the day Jesus was crucified for our sins.

The Bible says in Matthew 27:50, "And Jesus cried out again with a loud voice, and yielded up His spirit." Now stand in awe at the climactic response to the crucifixion of Jesus Christ:

> Then, behold, the veil of the temple was torn in two from top to bottom; and the earth quaked, and the rocks were split, and the graves were opened; and many bodies of the saints who had fallen asleep were raised; and coming out of the graves after His resurrection, they went into the holy city and appeared to many. (Matthew 27:51-53)

These historic and miraculous events both above the ground and beneath the earth rocked not only Jerusalem but the whole earth on that day of destiny. Jesus had just split the ground wide open!

The powers that had bound the saints of God could no longer hold them captive. Jesus was now handing over the reins of freedom to all those who would call upon His name. He had just issued a decree to all those who would call out to Him not only that day, but for all time to come (Romans 10:9-13).

Like the couriers in the book of Esther, our Father, the King, will press on and hasten to make sure that everyone knows that His Son Jesus has paid the ultimate price for us. We are indeed purchased, but not with the blood money that Haman had intended to give to all those who would have tried to destroy God's children. We were purchased with His priceless blood.

In that one solemn day we were redeemed and released into freedom. Jesus Christ did not purchase us with blood money but rather with His own royal blood. It was the blood of God's own Son.

After the decree was delivered, the despair of the Jewish people turned into a great celebration as they rejoiced in freedom.

> So Mordecai went out from the presence of the king in royal apparel of blue and white, with a great crown of gold and a garment of fine linen and purple; and the city of Shushan rejoiced and was glad. The Jews had light and gladness, joy and honor. And in every province and city, wherever the king's command and decree came, the Jews had joy and gladness, a feast and a holiday. Then many of the people of the land became Jews, because fear of the Jews fell upon them. (Esther 8:15-17)

You will remember a totally different scene back in Esther 3:15: "So the king and Haman sat down to drink, but the city of Shushan was perplexed." Shushan, under the decree of Haman, is a glimpse of what life is like without God.

When Satan is allowed to establish a stronghold in any town, group of people, or family there is deceit, confusion, anxiety, stress, hurt, anger and bitterness. Haman and the king had created wretched conditions for the people of Shushan.

Now a few months later the king, Esther, and Mordecai celebrate in Shushan. Because Esther and Mordecai had decreed life, there is now rejoicing in the city. The Jewish people were celebrating.

Observe the impact created by Esther and Mordecai in the last part of the verse in Esther 8:17: "Then many of the people of the land *became Jews*, because fear of the Jews fell upon them." The people who became Jews wanted to make it clear they were not the enemy of the Jews. Becoming a Jew allowed them to experience safety, honor, and gladness enjoyed by the Jewish people. Amazing!

Did you know that the presence of Christ in you could powerfully influence your neighbors? Did you know that you possess that kind of aura about you? His presence in us will create a hunger and thirst in others for Him so they too can live.

> For the love of Christ compels us, because we judge
> thus: that if One died for all, then all died; and He

died for all, that those who live should live no longer for themselves, but for Him who died for them and rose again. Therefore, from now on, we regard no one according to the flesh. Even though we have known Christ according to the flesh, yet now we know Him thus no longer. Therefore, if anyone is in Christ, he is a new creation; old things have passed away; behold, all things have become new. (2 Corinthians 5:14-17)

We close this chapter with the assurance that a proclamation of freedom has been declared over us. We are not victims any longer. Jesus Christ paid the ultimate price for our freedom on the cross on Mount Calvary. Just as the people of Shushan celebrated their freedom, we also can loudly proclaim our freedom. There is joy in the camp today.

—Ꮚᎇ *Chapter 9* ᎇᏊ—

You Write Your Own Decree (472 BC)

Chapter 8 ends in a climactic celebration by the Jewish people who had just been delivered from a state of emotional captivity and potential annihilation. A feast and a national holiday had been declared to celebrate their quickly gained freedom.

After enduring several agonizing months of emotional torture expecting to be murdered by their enemies, the Jewish people suddenly were granted power and authority to defend themselves. Imagine the shouts of jubilation that began to spring up all across the king's one hundred and twenty-seven provinces as each province received word of their new empowerment.

Now envision the shock and terror that gripped the hearts of the Persians and Medes people as they learned that the new decree stipulated that the Jews could destroy, kill, and annihilate all the forces of any people that intended to harm them.

Enemies of the Jewish people quickly abandoned any plan to collect the bounty of ten thousand talents of silver placed on the head of each Jew killed. Chapter 8 ends with "many of the people of the land became Jews, because fear of the Jews fell upon them" (Esther 8:17).

Not only did the general population of Persians and Medes grasp the implication of the Jews being granted authority to defend themselves, but also the government officials. They quickly jumped on the bandwagon and took sides with the Jews.

> And all the officials of the provinces, the satraps, the governors, and all those doing the king's work, helped the Jews, because the fear of Mordecai fell upon them. For Mordecai was great in the king's palace, and his fame spread throughout all the provinces; for this man Mordecai became increasingly prominent. (Esther 9:3-4)

In this rapid turn of events the government's political support was reversed and now supported the Jews. Although there was a previous decree that had been written and signed by the king through the influence of Haman to annihilate the Jews, the government now endorsed Mordecai's decree.

These two opposing decrees forced people and officials to choose sides. Would they side with the now defeated Haman and his sons? Or would they side with Mordecai and Esther and support the Jews? We know from Esther 8:17 that many chose to switch sides and stand with Mordecai because of fear.

On the thirteenth day of the twelfth month of Adar, Esther 9:5 says, "Thus the Jews defeated all their enemies with the stroke of the sword, with slaughter and destruction, and did what they pleased with those who hated them."

Seizing the opportunity granted them by King Ahasuerus through Mordecai's decree, the Jews relentlessly pursued the enemy. Attacking the capital city of Shushan the citadel, the Jews killed and destroyed five hundred men (Esther 9:6).

At the end of the day the number of all those killed in the citadel was reported to the king. The king relays this report to Queen Esther and informs her that the ten sons of her enemy, Haman, have also been killed. The king then asks Queen Esther a question that demonstrates his concern for all those in his kingdom.

"What have they done in the rest of the king's provinces?" (Esther 9:12) Realizing that five hundred of the enemy have been killed in the citadel right within his sight, the king wants to know what else needs to be done in the kingdom outside of his sight.

Do you ever feel like you are in the battle all alone? Do you often believe you are the only one carrying the Sword of Truth, engaging the enemy all by yourself?

We would do well today to consider the same question that the king asked Esther. It is very encouraging to realize that there is a vast array of soldiers of the Cross who are committed to their destiny in the world today, each boldly marching forward in the name of the King of Kings!

The king asked Esther, "Now what is your petition? It shall be granted to you. Or what is your further request? It shall be done" (Esther 9:12).

Queen Esther responded in verse thirteen by requesting the king to allow an additional day of battle for the Jews in Shushan. Take notice she asked for a second day of battle to take place only within the citadel, Shushan, but not outside the capital city.

My first instinct was to wonder why Esther wanted more bloodshed after the victory in Shushan. After considerable reflection, one of several thoughts came to me.

Shushan was the headquarters of all the activity of the entire one hundred twenty-seven provinces of the king. I think Queen Esther believed it was imperative that a strong message be sent throughout the kingdom concerning her people, the Jews.

By thoroughly destroying the enemy in Shushan the citadel, all the Jews throughout all the provinces would be strongly encouraged to pursue and destroy the enemy in their province. Esther's brave response crushed the will and resistance of the enemy.

While we may not be able to prevent the fiery darts of the enemy from being thrown at us, God has thoroughly equipped us to defend our faith and defeat our enemy, Satan.

Esther's firm response ensured that any remnant of Haman's evil influence or any allegiance to his plot was stamped out. Her decisive actions confirmed publicly the support for the Jews.

In addition to Esther asking the king for one more day of war, she also added a very unusual request. Esther requested that Haman's ten dead sons be hanged on the gallows. What? Hang ten dead men? Why?

The answer may be found in the definition of gallows:

> gallows ~ a wooden structure where people used to hang criminals or enemies in order to kill them. Or, a wooden structure where people would hang the dead bodies of criminals or enemies.[1]

We could speculate that Esther's motive for this unusual request was to publicly assure the Jews and other citizens that the reign of terror from Haman and his sons was terminated. All citizens were now free from harm if they stood with the Jews, God's people.

While the above motive makes sense, I still wondered if I was missing something concerning the ten sons. Why make such a public spectacle other than to firmly demonstrate the kingdom was now free of Haman's family? What else could be so important that Esther petitioned the king to hang the ten dead sons of Haman on the gallows in Shushan?

As I contemplated these questions, it occurred to me that 2 Timothy 3:16 tells us that all scripture is inspired by God.

Clearly God intentionally had the author of the book of Esther list all ten sons of Haman by name as found in Esther 9:7-10.

Continuing my research, I felt impressed to investigate whether the names of each son had a particular meaning. In Bible days, specific meanings and significance were attached to names of individuals. This tradition is still practiced today.

My investigation into the meaning of the names of Haman's ten sons proved interesting. I researched a Judaism question and answer site entitled "Mi Yodeya" which is found in the StackExchange website. It should not be taken as final authority, nor as a replacement of your own research. However, I did find it personally revealing as related to the nature of Satan. I have listed the brief meaning attached to each of their names:

1. Parshandatha – an interpreter of the law and one who distances himself from the Torah (the Jewish written law)
2. Dalphon – "house of caves" or a person with wrong intentions
3. Aspatha – "gathering" or a person who accumulates money and has no time left to study the Torah
4. Poratha – a person who desires to gaze at uncovered women
5. Adalia – lifted up, feelings of haughtiness and arrogance
6. Aridatha – an evil inclination distracting a person from praying fervently like a lion

7. Parmashta – it rips apart the strong connection (literally the crisscross of a garment) that exists between fellow Jews

8. Arisai – it continuously poisons a person with snake's venom

9. Aridai – the evil that paralyzes a righteous person with worry about his livelihood, and causes suffering

10. Vajezatha – the bitterness of the olive, symbolizing bitter and strong judgement[2]

This investigative diversion confirmed to me there is significance in a person's name. The evil inclinations and character of each son had already been exposed and confirmed by their own name.

One of these days each redeemed child of God will receive a personal and unique name from God. Revelation 2:17 says, "He who has an ear, let him hear what the Spirit says to the churches. To him who overcomes I will give some of the hidden manna to eat. And I will give him a white stone, and on the stone a new name written which no one knows except him who receives it."

This captivating revelation from God creates more questions than answers. Regardless of God's motive or purpose in giving each of His redeemed children a new name, this special recognition discloses His personal relationship that He desires to have with each one of His children.

Retracing our steps back to Esther's petition of the king, let us examine in greater depth the motive for her request to hang the ten dead sons of Haman. As suggested earlier, the following may represent some of her motive:

- By thoroughly destroying the enemy in the capital city of Shushan, Esther crushed the will of anyone attempting to continue evil intentions against her people, the Jews.
- By publicly hanging the ten dead sons of Haman, Esther dramatically exposed the evil intentions of Haman and assured the kingdom that his wicked plot was terminated.

Esther had asked the king to allow the Jews to continue to destroy the enemy in Shushan an additional day. The king granted her request and another three hundred men of Shushan were killed on the fourteenth day.

Earlier it was reported that on the thirteenth day they had killed five hundred men in Shushan. Now there were a total of eight hundred men killed in Shushan. Even though the Jews were authorized by the king in Esther 8:11 to plunder the enemy's possessions, they did not lay a hand on the plunder.

"The remainder of the Jews in the king's provinces gathered together and protected their lives, had rest from their enemies, and killed seventy-five thousand of their enemies; but they did not lay a hand on the plunder." (Esther 9:16)

The Jews outside of Shushan rested on the fourteenth day while their fellow Jews continued the destruction of the enemy within Shushan. The next day, the fifteenth day of the month of Adar, the Jews within the citadel rested. These two days of rest were declared holidays, days of feasting and gladness, as declared in Esther 9:20-22.

If you want to add salt to an open wound, write a decree to celebrate your victory over your enemies every year!

Refer to Esther 9:20-32. Esther 9:28 declares, "that these days should be remembered and kept throughout every generation, every family, every province, and every city, that these days of Purim should not fail to be observed among the Jews, and that the memory of them should not perish among their descendants."

I would be remiss concluding this chapter if I did not discuss the issue of plunder. In the third chapter of Esther, Haman told the Medes and Persians they would receive ten thousand talents of silver for each Jew that they killed. They were told to plunder the Jews possessions as well.

Although Esther and Mordecai wrote it into their letters of decree to "plunder their possessions" (Esther 8:11), please note that the Jews did not lay a hand on the plunder of the Persians and Medes. Why not? It was certainly authorized.

Speculation as to why the Jews did not lay a hand on the plunder is as follows:

- The Jews were attempting to right a wrong that had been committed by King Saul years earlier. Saul was commanded by God through the prophet Samuel to *not* touch the plunder of the Amalekites. King Saul disobeyed and allowed his men to take the plunder of the best of the spoils and even took King Agag alive (1 Samuel 15). Haman was a descendent of Agag.

• The Jews only wanted to destroy their enemy and they desired nothing from them. Perhaps they refused to have any plunder within their walls as they may have believed that God would declare them unclean by possessing unclean plunder.

The attitude of the Jews toward evil plunder serves as a pattern for Christians to follow today. We dare not contaminate our hearts and minds with Satan's evil plunder. God commands us to flee the very appearance of evil. "Abstain from every form of evil. Now may the God of peace Himself sanctify you completely; and may your whole spirit, soul, and body be preserved blameless at the coming of our Lord Jesus Christ." (1 Thessalonians 5:22-23)

Chapter 10

Seeking Good and Speaking Peace (472 BC)

Back in chapter 8 we saw a young, shy Queen Esther who had timidly approached King Ahasuerus with her request to save her Jewish people from annihilation. The king reminded Esther that he had already taken off his signet ring, which he had removed from Haman, and given it to Mordecai. The king had also awarded Esther full ownership of the house of Haman.

Esther had not recognized the significance of what the king had already given to her. With possession of the ring and the ownership of the house of Haman, Mordecai and Esther now had full authority of the king to make their own decrees.

"Then Queen Esther, …, wrote with full authority to confirm this second letter about Purim." (Esther 9:29) What a different and confident woman we now see in Queen Esther.

Today we must likewise recognize that God has already equipped us through the power of the Holy Spirit to achieve our destiny.

Chapter 9 ends with decrees declared by Queen Esther and Mordecai. They wrote letters to the Jewish people to confirm the days of Purim, after the name of Pur, or the lot. Purim is the name given to the holiday on the fourteenth and fifteenth day of the month of Adar, which called for two days of feasting and gladness.

What a shock and surprise transpired when the Medes and Persians first heard of the new decree by Esther and Mordecai. They certainly did not see that coming. Quickly the new decree was being spread and their destruction was imminent.

> Watch therefore, for you do not know what hour your Lord is coming. But know this, that if the master of the house had known what hour the thief would come, he would have watched and not allowed his house to be broken into. Therefore you also be ready, for the Son of Man is coming at an hour you do not expect. (Matthew 24:42-44)

These Scriptures warn us of the imminent return of Jesus Christ. No one knows the date, but signs of the time tell us that it is very soon. We must be prepared and ready for His return.

As news of the new decree spread rapidly, fear gripped the hearts of many Persians and Medes as they recognized their lives were in grave danger. They needed to quickly convert their way of thinking, their way of life, and their words if they wanted to live (Esther 8:17).

God has issued us a new decree in giving us His Son, Jesus Christ, as redemption for our sins. Just like the Medes and Persians, we must immediately turn from our way of thinking, our way of life, and our words, and surrender our will to His will.

As we enter into the last chapter of the book of Esther, we discover that chapter 10, while comprised of only three verses, has the makings of a perfect ending to this dramatic story of divine destiny.

Esther 10:1 tells us that King Ahasuerus imposed a tribute, or tax, upon all the kingdom. This imposition of tax symbolized the king's power and authority over the people of his kingdom.

The king was requiring the people to return to him a portion of their livelihood in exchange for protection and services provided by his government. This taxation created an expectation from the people that they were now included in the house of the king.

As I read this verse where the king required tribute from the people in his kingdom, please allow me to briefly digress. I was reminded that God also requires something from His children to be returned to Him. God's tribute is called tithes.

God tells us to return ten percent of our increase, or tithes, back to Him. All that we have is already His by right of divine ownership. When we obey Him in returning the tithe, God promises a blessing.

'Bring all the tithes into the storehouse, that there may be food in My house, and try Me now in this,' says the Lord of hosts, 'If I will not open for you the windows of heaven and pour out for you such blessing that there will not be room enough to receive it. And I will rebuke the devourer for your sakes, so that he will not destroy the fruit of your ground, nor shall the vine fail to bear fruit for you in the field,' says the Lord of hosts; 'and all nations will call you blessed, for you will be a delightful land,' says the Lord of hosts. (Malachi 3:10-12)

God promises to provide and protect all His children who obey Him in the principle of returning the tithe. He dares each of us to try Him now in this single act of obedience.

Returning to the story, we read of Mordecai's accomplishments in Esther 10:2: "Now all the acts of his power and his might, and the account of the greatness of Mordecai, to which the king advanced him, are they not written in the book of the chronicles of the kings of Media and Persia?"

Earlier in chapter 2 we discovered how Mordecai saved the king's life by informing Esther of a plot he had overheard between two of the king's servants. The account of Mordecai's brave action was recorded in the book of the chronicles.

Later in chapter 6 of Esther we read that King Ahasuerus was having difficulty falling asleep. Calling for his servant, the king commanded the book of the chronicles be read to him.

It was not by mere coincidence that the servant began to read of the account of the brave Jew named Mordecai who had saved the king's life some five years earlier. Divine destiny brought together a restless king and the report of a courageous deed by Mordecai that ultimately saved the Jewish race.

Honoring Mordecai for his valor, the king later removed the royal robe and signet ring from Haman and presented them to Mordecai. In the end, justice was served.

Looking at Esther 10:2 closer, we catch a glimpse of how God faithfully keeps this story alive today. God has the last word in everything, including the book of the chronicles. It was simply divine destiny that arranged this significant Biblical historical story to be recorded in the book of the chronicles of the kings of Media and Persia.

If Esther and Mordecai had failed to fulfill their destiny, the king's book of the chronicles would have read much differently. The death of Mordecai on the gallows and the annihilation of the Jewish race would have been the headlines. God intervened and the books were written to record a victorious end. God only writes great finishes for His children!

"For Mordecai the Jew was second to King Ahasuerus, and was great among the Jews and well received by the multitude of his brethren, seeking the good of his people and speaking peace to all his countrymen." (Esther 10:3)

Mordecai's promotion to second in command demonstrates that God bestows great blessing on those who obey Him. He was widely respected throughout the kingdom because the people recognized his love for their welfare and safety.

God placed Mordecai in a position of great responsibility. He could have easily abused his power to exact revenge on other non-Jewish races within the kingdom. Rather than abuse his position, Mordecai exercised his authority to create a safe environment for all the people. His example is a reflection of how God ministers to all His children of all races. Much like Mordecai, we are to love and care for one another.

God created you and He desires to cultivate an intimate relationship with you. His unending love for you is absolutely unconditional. Surrender your will to His destiny for you.

As we conclude our study of the book of Esther, it must be stated that only God could conceive and produce the perfect ending to a perfect story. Your ending to your story will also be perfect as you seek His divine destiny for your life.

Your destiny is the mosaic in God's landscape of love.

☞ Chapter 11 ☜

Last Words, Today's Timeline

As you reflect on what you have read and learned from this brief but compelling book of Esther, you will draw the conclusion as I did that this book was not just randomly included in the Old Testament. The Holy Spirit inspired the author to write about these events and persons to convey God's message that He has designed a divine destiny for each one of us.

God has blessed me with this opportunity and responsibility to share in written form what He has revealed to me through this thorough study of Esther. It is more than just a good story. This book of Esther is the blueprint for the path to our destiny.

Your Bible is a goldmine revealing precious golden nuggets from our Father. Digging out these golden nuggets requires extensive time and exhaustive effort. I challenge you today to immerse yourself in the Word of God and uncover these jewels that will enhance your spiritual growth and develop your understanding.

As a child of God, I want to know and understand what my heavenly Father is telling me through His Word. Do you want to have the Word of God revealed to your spirit? Study rigorously the Word with your spiritual eyes and with an open heart. God will begin to reveal to you the mysteries that are known only to Him. He loves to reveal His Word to His children.

We do not know all the people of the world by name, but we know their destiny. To those who choose not to follow Christ, they will one day look up with anguish in their tear stained eyes and remember the opportunities and the many times that God stood knocking at the door of their heart. He still knocks at your heart's door today if you will listen.

"Behold, I stand at the door and knock. If anyone hears My voice and opens the door, I will come in to him and dine with him, and he with Me." (Revelation 3:20) This personal invitation in scripture comes directly from Jesus Christ who died for you.

The hour is late. The Lamb's Book of Life is being written now. Is your name written in The Lamb's Book of Life? If not, I invite you today to make sure of your own *eternal destiny*.

Step 1: Ask Jesus to forgive you of your sins.

Step 2: Ask Jesus to come into your life.

Step 3: Begin to receive Him as Savior, Lord, and King today.

Step 4: Begin to worship Him.

Step 5: Begin to read the Word of God, the Bible.

Crave the Word of God more than life itself. God will begin to introduce Himself to you as you step out in faith to know Him personally.

I encourage you to pick up my Christian study book, *Echoes from God: For Growing Deep, Growing Strong in the Faith.* You will begin to learn in a simple, but personal, way what God wants to show you about your new relationship with Him.

If your name is written in the Lamb's Book of Life, then I encourage you with the words Paul wrote to the Philippians.

> Rejoice in the Lord always. Again I will say, rejoice! Let your gentleness be known to all men. The Lord is at hand. Be anxious for nothing, but in everything by prayer and supplication, with thanksgiving, let your requests be made known to God; and the peace of God, which surpasses all understanding, will guard your hearts and minds through Christ Jesus. (Philippians 4:4-7)

The Long, Long Night

The Story of Destiny

STUDY GUIDE

Reflections
and Talking Points

Preface

Personal Reflections Work Sheet

As you reflect back upon your responses to this work sheet, understand that God will intertwine the events of your life in such a way as to make you the vessel that He can use for *such a time as this*. But, you must stay submissive to His will and stay melted like wax before Him. Do not let the struggles of your life harden you. Many of these struggles were set in motion to shape you for His perfect plan for your life; your destiny. Your life is *bigger than you*. You may be the one He is using for planting the seed for the next generation's leader. Trust Him; He knows *your* destiny.

1. Where were you born?

2. How old were you when you were born into the Kingdom of God?

3. List some joyous occasions in your life…

4. List some struggles in your life….

5. Describe how God has used your joys and struggles to form who you are today.

6. Of all your joys and struggles, which ones shaped you the most to be who/what you are today?

7. What are the struggles of your past that God has shown to you that you now realize you need to let go of in order to move forward toward your destiny?

8. Looking back upon your joys and struggles, were they for a one-time purpose in your life or for a lifetime of shaping and molding?

9. What is God's plan or purpose for your life?

Talking Points

Chapter 1: The Queen Said "NO!" (483 BC)

1. Why was Queen Vashti removed from her throne?

2. "Then he sent letters to all the king's provinces, to each province in its own script, and to every people in their own language, that each man should be master in his own house, and speak in the language of his own people." (Esther 1:22)
    What possible effects could this decree have upon the marriages in the king's provinces?

Chapter 2: The Installation of Queen Esther (478 BC)

1. Why is it important for the reader to know about the lineage of Mordecai and Esther? (Refer to Esther 2:5-7, 10, 20.)

2. Discuss what may have transpired in the four or five years between the removal of Queen Vashti and the crowning of Queen Esther.

3. Describe the process of selecting Esther as the new queen.

4. What turn of events resulted in Mordecai's name being recorded in the king's book of chronicles? (Refer to Esther 2:21-23.)

5. How would you feel if your only reward for saving the king's life was to have your name recorded within his book of chronicles?

Chapter 3: Haman's Great Revenge (474 BC)

1. What was the servants' response to Mordecai not bowing to Haman?

2. Why was Mordecai so determined to annihilate an entire Jewish race versus simply punishing Mordecai, the Jew?

3. What was the lineage of Haman? (1 Samuel 15:32-33 and Esther 3:1)

4. Discuss the emotions that might have been felt by the Jews as they waited out the eleven long months for their decreed annihilation.

5. When and how did Haman get the king's signet ring?

6. "But the city of Shushan was perplexed." (Esther 3:15) Why was the city perplexed over these events?

Chapter 4: If I Perish, I Perish (473 BC)

1. Discuss reasons Esther was asking for information regarding the what and why of Mordecai's mourning (Esther 4:5).

2. Contrast the prevention of the annihilation of the Jewish race, which is the reason for Queen Esther's fasting and prayers, with the preservation of the birth of the Messiah.

Chapter 5: If It Pleases the King (473 BC)

1. In chapter 5 of Esther, the queen is given several opportunities to tell the king of the plans for the annihilation of her people, the Jews. What was Esther's motive for inviting the king and Haman to her house for a banquet?

2. What was the characteristic portrayed by Haman that God hates? Read Proverbs 8:13; 16:18; and Psalm 10:4 for talking points.

Chapter 6: The Long, Long Night (473 BC)

1. Discuss how God's timing is not always man's timing. Use the example of Mordecai finally getting the proper recognition five years later for his act of bravery as your talking point.

2. Discuss how Haman's world begins to crumble when he learns of the king's desire to honor Mordecai.

3. Esther requests the king and Haman to return to her house for a second banquet. During the *long, long night* between the banquets the gallows are being constructed and the king is having difficulty sleeping. Discuss any connections you may see between the gallows and the king's restless night. (Refer to Esther 5:13-14; 6:1-3.)

Chapter 7: Haman is Hanged (473 BC)

1. The king asked Esther *who* is he and *where* is he who would dare to harm his queen. Discuss how Jesus might ask this same question concerning Satan attempting to harm His bride.

2. Discuss your thoughts on Haman being hanged on the same gallows he had constructed for the death of Mordecai.

Chapter 8: The King's Decree and the Signet Ring (473 BC)

1. "So the king took off his signet ring, which he had taken from Haman, and gave it to Mordecai; and Esther appointed Mordecai over the house of Haman." (Esther 8:2) Discuss the change of power that took place and how it is reflected within this one verse.

2. Esther returns to the king for yet another petition. This time she came back to save the entire Jewish race. Recall that the king had already given to Mordecai and Esther all that he had taken back from Haman: the house, the robe, and the signet ring. Discuss why the king told them to write their own decree.

3. Contrast the difference between the city of Shushan as recorded earlier in Esther 3:15 and now in Esther 8:15.

Chapter 9: You Write Your Own Decree (472 BC)

1. Discuss how the timing of God's answer to our prayer may be different from what we expect.

2. Discuss Esther's motive for requesting a second day of battle only within the city of Shushan.

3. Discuss the significance of the hanging of the ten sons of Haman who were already dead.

4. I have discussed the meanings of the names of Haman's ten sons in chapter 9. These names were quickly found on the internet. There are also meanings for many of the other names that are contained in the book of Esther. You might find it interesting to do your own search of these names. These searches would make lively talking points.

Chapter 10: Seeking Good and Speaking Peace (472 BC)

1. As disciples of Christ, discuss how we can seek the good of our people and speak peace to our countrymen.

2. Discuss how you see God weaving your destiny into His landscape of love.

Concluding Prayer

If you do not have a personal relationship with the Lord Jesus Christ, I challenge you today to ask Jesus into your heart and begin to serve Him. He has already written a decree for your life, one filled with great plans.

"For I know the thoughts that I think toward you, says the LORD, thoughts of peace and not of evil, to give you a future and a hope." (Jeremiah 29:11)

Please pray this simple prayer and watch God take over your life and bring you joy like you have never known.

> *Dear Jesus, please forgive me of my sins. I acknowledge that You are the One who paid in full for my sins upon the cross of Calvary. I confess that You are the Son of the living God.*
>
> *I ask You to come into my heart and be my Savior and Lord. I submit my will and my life to You. I will serve You as my Savior and Lord from this day forward all the days of my life.*
>
> *Amen.*

If you prayed that prayer, Jesus heard your prayer today and He came into your heart. He has been waiting for your invitation. Become a student of the Word of God through daily reading of the Bible. You will find so many of your life's questions are answered in the scriptures. The Holy Spirit will enter your life and become your teacher, your guide, and your comforter.

I encourage you to read the following verses as a start today.

John 3:16-17; Romans 10:8-13; and John 14:26

If you have accepted Christ as your Savior and Lord today, then I encourage you to pick up my Christian study book, *Echoes from God: For Growing Deep, Growing Strong in the Faith*. It will be a great resource for your Christian growth.

Notes

Introduction

1. "Esther," Bible Hub. 2004, http:// biblehub.com/timeline/ esther/1.htm
2. Dawson, Joy A., introduction to "The Book of Esther." In *The Spirit Filled Life Bible*, ed. by Jack Hayford (Nashville: Thomas Nelson, 2002), 632.
3. Wikipedia contributors, "Memucan," *Wikipedia, The Free Encyclopedia*, https://en.wikipedia.org/w/index. php?title=Memucan&oldid=664627611 (accessed August 29, 2016).

Chapter 1: The Queen Said "NO!" (483 BC)

1. *Wikipedia*, s.v. "Memucan," last modified May 29, 2015, https:// en.wikipedia.org/wiki/Memucan.
2. Ibid.

Chapter 2: The Installation of Queen Esther (478 BC)

1. Wikipedia contributors, "Myrrh," *Wikipedia, The Free Encyclopedia*, https://en.wikipedia.org/w/index. php?title=Myrrh&oldid=736714415 (accessed August 29, 2016).

Chapter 9: You Write Your Own Decree (472 BC)

1. Bryce, Robert, "God Is in Control", found in Word List. February 2006, http://www.easyenglish.info/bible-commentary/esther-lbw.htm.
2. "Mi Yodeya", Last modified February 11, 2014, http://judaism.stackexchange.com/questions/28326/what-meaning-do-the-names-of-the-ten-sons-of-haman-have.

About the Author

International speaker, TV and radio minister, author, and artist Dee Levens is a retired school administrator and now finds herself engaged in full-time ministry. Dee and her husband, Jack, have two daughters, two sons-in-law, and six grandchildren, who all add a great deal of joy to her life.

This is Dee's second book. Her first book, *Echoes from God: For Growing Deep, Growing Strong in the Faith,* has been gifted to over six thousand pastors in Kenya and Uganda. These books were gifted while she was conducting crusades for pastors in Africa. Dee's desire is to get the Word of God to as many people as she can through these various ministry opportunities.